OWN YOUR GAME

ALSO BY DAVE STOCKTON

Unconscious Putting
Unconscious Scoring

OWN YOUR GAME

HOW TO USE YOUR MIND TO PLAY WINNING GOLF

DAVE STOCKTON
WITH MATTHEW RUDY

GOTHAM BOOKS

GOTHAM BOOKS
Published by the Penguin Group
Penguin Group (USA) LLC
375 Hudson Street
New York, New York 10014

USA | Canada | UK | Ireland | Australia | New Zealand | India | South Africa | China
penguin.com
A Penguin Random House Company

LIBRARY OF CONGRESS CATALOGING-IN-PUBLICATION DATA
Stockton, Dave.
Own your game : how to use your mind to play winning golf / Dave Stockton, Matthew Rudy.
pages cm.
ISBN 978-1-592-40851-1 (hardback)
1. Golf—Training. 2. Golf—Psychological aspects. I. Rudy, Matthew. II. Title.
GV979.T68S82 2014
796.35201'9—dc23
2013034051

Printed in the United States of America
1 3 5 7 9 10 8 6 4 2

Set in Adobe Garamond
Designed by Spring Hoteling

For the Stockton family, who have given me so much guidance and support over the years—Gail (above), Audrey,
Cathy, Dave Jr., and Ron.

TABLE OF CONTENTS

OWN YOUR GAME

FOREWORD

I first got to know Dave Stockton during the PGA Tour season leading up to the 1991 Ryder Cup. Dave was the captain of the American team, and he spent that year familiarizing himself with the players who could potentially be on his team. He wanted to understand our likes and dislikes and to put us in the best position to play well at Kiawah Island that fall. We saw him a lot out on tour throughout the season, watching how we responded to playing with different guys and getting our feedback.

Dave was truly an all-inclusive captain. He surrounded himself with people he thought could help him, and he made winning the Cup a full team effort. When you're a captain, that's the best you can do. The players have to go out and hit the shots, but when we played with Dave, we never felt like we were alone. He's naturally likable, and he commands respect—but he doesn't demand it, which is a totally different thing.

As captain for the 2008 matches, I came from outside the box in terms of team building and used a different approach than he did. But I asked Dave to be my assistant because I knew he'd be a tremendous asset. I valued his opinion, and I knew he would tell me the truth. It was also important for an entire generation of players who might not have been familiar with Dave to be able to spend some time with him and learn from him.

The fortunate group of current players who work with Dave are getting the benefit of his expertise, experience and skill at sharing what he knows. Dave is a creative thinker, and he sees things others don't. He's very bright and articulate, and he has his finger on the pulse of what it takes to play at the highest level. When he's working with you, he listens to what you have to say about your game, he evaluates what he sees, and he helps you find what's missing. There's no "my way or the highway" with him, and no ego. He values the input of others—and that's an important instructional quality.

Dave is an example of somebody who has made the most out of what was God-given to him. He knew that mental strength was a quality required for success, and he cultivated that in himself. Dave has had a long and successful career, winning two majors on the PGA Tour and three as a senior golfer—and we were proud to win that 1991 Ryder Cup with him as our captain. He and his sons are making a huge impact working with tour players around the world.

But most importantly, Dave Stockton is the kind of guy who would do anything for a friend—or even somebody he's never met. Dave gives his time, which is the most valuable thing we all have to give. Not many people know this, but when I was going through cancer treatments in 1994, I needed five weeks of radiation therapy in Loma Linda, California. Dave lives very close, in Redlands. He and his wife, Cathy, moved out of their beautiful house for five weeks so I could stay there with my wife and kids and get that treatment.

We couldn't be more grateful for the kindness Dave has always shown, and I love seeing the success he's having. He deserves it.

Paul Azinger
Major championship winner
and 2008 Ryder Cup Captain

Bradenton, Florida

August 15, 2013

PREFACE

WHEN the Congressional Medal of Honor Society had one of its biennial meetings in Riverside, California, in the early 2000s, one of my jobs as a board member was to try to make sure our meeting guests felt welcome.

I walked over to a very nice-looking couple and introduced myself, and the man said he was Dave Stockton. I said, "Wow, just like the golfer." Dave gave me a smile, and said "I play golf." For the rest of the night, I introduced Dave to some of our other society members as the "imposter" Dave Stockton, getting a good laugh each time and making a friend in the process. Little did I know just how important Dave would become to some causes I feel very strongly about.

We all have stories of friendly people we meet at business meetings. You exchange business cards and make a vague promise to meet up down the road. You don't actually expect it to happen. But Dave asked me where I was from that night, and I told him I lived in Tampa and gave him my card. He gave me his card and said he was playing in an event near there later that year, and that he'd give me a call when he was in town. Sure enough, six months later, my phone rings and it's Dave.

He does what he says he's going to do.

That was the beginning of a wonderful relationship with Dave and the entire "Team Stockton." With Dave's help, we started the annual Medal of Honor Golf Classic, which has raised tens of thousands of dollars for the Society and various other charities. Without support from Dave and his family, there would be no tournament. It's that simple. He's an incredible partner.

I have the utmost respect for Dave. He's in there with you. He makes you feel like home when you're with him. I'm honored to call him my close friend—and it's a testament to Dave that probably 800,000 people in the world feel the same.

He's just that way.

The Honorable Ronald E. Ray
Former Assistant Secretary of Veterans Affairs

Medal of Honor Recipient, 1970
Former President, Congressional
Medal of Honor Society

INTRODUCTION

HOW do you work on your golf game?

That might sound like a silly question. Most players I've met take about four seconds to think about it and answer one of two ways. They either say they use some combination of hitting balls, taking lessons and reading or watching instruction tips, or they say they don't do much besides go out and play.

Hearing those answers, I'm not surprised so many players tread water at the same handicap level for years. Sure, they might get lucky, make a few putts and make a career score once every couple of summers, but they mostly just hover in their comfort zone.

Tour players obviously play the game at a different level, but they follow the same pattern. A lot of them do a ton of work on the mechanical parts of their game—watching hours of video with a swing coach to get in all the right positions. Then they go out and hit thousands of balls. But all of that physical labor is usually not enough to push their game to the next level. It doesn't turn a fringe tour player into a winner, or a winner into a major championship contender.

I'm not saying you don't need to know the basics of how to hold a club or how to swing it. Mechanical instruction has a place in the game—whether you're a beginner or a tour player.

But the biggest missing piece for all of those players doesn't have anything to do with mechanics or fundamentals.

It's the mental component.

The way you use your mind ultimately determines how well you're going to play. You can have all the mechanical information and training in the world, but if you can't prepare yourself mentally to play, make the right decisions for your own personal game and situation when you're out there, and understand and handle your emotions, it will be very hard to get any better than you are right now.

That might sound harsh, but it should be liberating. You don't have to be a monster physical specimen and hit three hundred range balls a day to be a good player. You don't have to have a perfect swing. And you don't have to hit great shots all the time—or even most of the time.

You just need to think a little better. Anybody can do it, and I'm going to show you how.

Every couple of weeks during the PGA Tour season, I'll get a phone call from a player, agent, or caddie asking me or my sons and coaching partners, Dave Jr. and Ron, to help fix somebody's putting or short-game issue. We'll set up a time to meet—usually at one of my home courses in California. This is a player's livelihood we're talking about, and almost all of them take the process very seriously—to the point where they tell me they've cleared a bunch of time over two days to work really intensively.

I can understand that, but it never takes that long.

Let me give you an example.

A few years ago, J. B. Holmes called me up and asked me to help him with his putting. He flew in early, but his bags didn't make it. He was using the long putter at the time—which I wasn't aware of—but for the hour we were on the practice green before his clubs came, he used my standard putter. We didn't talk anything about mechanics. I just watched him go through his routine and roll some putts. I asked him what his routine was when he hit his driver, and he described a quick, decisive process. Then I watched him get slow and deliberate over his putt, looking at it from every angle as if his life depended on every piece of information he could find. He was really struggling—virtually every player who goes to the long putter is—and he honestly believed he wasn't a good putter.

But you don't hit the ball as far as J.B. does without athletic ability and a great pair of hands. He has tremendous coordination and touch. There was no reason he couldn't putt great. We talked about changing his routine so that he simply painted a quick picture in his mind of where he thought the ball was going to go and he copied the picture with how he rolled the ball.

In the last half hour with the regular putter, he rolled the ball great. Then his bag showed up, and he pulled out the long putter he had been using. It was heavy and clumsy—and he had been told it fit him perfectly. He proceeded to basically whiff it the first four or five times. He tossed the long putter away, took my putter back and immediately got back to rolling it great. He took that putter with him and proceeded to make twenty-four of twenty-six cuts and have the best season of his career.

I can understand how a weekend player might be skeptical about just how much a change in mental approach could improve his or her scores. For a tour player, improving by one shot per round can be the difference between making the FedEx Cup playoffs at the end of the season and getting demoted to the Web.com Tour. If you're shooting 97 every day, getting to the low 80s seems like forever away.

But I can tell you that from working with 90- and 100-shooters for decades in clinics and pro-ams, it really is that simple. If you and I rode in a cart together for your next round of golf, I could improve your score by four or five shots immediately, just by helping you see the shots you should be hitting instead of the ones you're actually considering. And once you've taken the time to digest everything in this book, your handicap and enjoyment of the game will only continue to improve.

Instead of grinding away at the range, trying to find the magic formula that will make your swing work that day or that week, you'll learn how to visualize what you want to do and play with confidence instead of tension. Instead of obsessing about hitting every shot perfectly, you'll learn how to play the shot in front of you and pick the right shots and strategies for your skills.

Golf is going to be fun again.

I know that when a lot of players think about golf instruction, they immediately start looking for a bunch of photographs and diagrams. They want somebody to tell them exactly what grip to use, how many inches to take the putter back for a certain length putt, what drills to do for a particular day of the week and how many times to do them.

If you've heard anything about how I teach—or if you've read either of my last two books, *Unconscious Putting* and *Unconscious Scoring*—you know that the Stockton Golf approach is different.

This book is, too.

We're going to talk about how to use your mind to play better with the game you have. You won't see any diagrams or read any discussions about how far apart your feet should be on a chip shot versus a pitch shot.

I'm going to share the secrets to a tour-caliber mental game I've learned from more than fifty years as a competitive player at the game's highest level, more than forty-five years as an instructor, and my time as captain in the high-stress environment of the Ryder Cup. The lessons I learned from the great teachers and players from the 1950s through to today—teachers like my dad, Gail, John St. Clair, Paul Runyan, Harvey Penick, Chuck Cook, Jim Flick and Mac O'Grady, and players like Julius Boros, Jack Nicklaus, Arnold Palmer, Billy Casper, Lee Trevino, Gary Player, Rory McIlroy, Al Geiberger, Don January, Phil Mickelson and many others. Strategies that my sons and I help players develop every week out on the professional tours.

To begin the book, I'll use Chapter 1 to take you inside the ropes at the biggest events in the pro game and show you exactly how skills like confidence, calmness, and focus make the difference between winning and losing in a group where everybody has tremendous physical talent. You'll see that the higher your handicap is, the more potential you have for improvement. Simply put, you can think your way to your career round—today. In Chapter 2, we'll talk about the myth of "trying," and why grinding over more and more practice shots at the range and taking that extra breath and practice swing before a must-have tee shot are dooming you to struggle.

In Chapter 3, I'll show you how the best players handle pressure—however you define it. Whether you're trying to win the club championship, break 80 for the first time, or make your first birdie, you'll have a better chance to succeed—immediately—when you learn how to approach those situations the same way you would any other shot. It's not magic. It comes from creating a routine that fits you.

By now, it's probably clear that I believe 90 percent of this game is mental—and any work you do on the mental side is going to have much more impact on your score. That doesn't mean there's no place in the game for improving your physical skills. But to get any value out of instruction—whether it's mental or physical—you have to be able to know what advice suits you and how to apply it to yourself. In Chapter 4, I'll show you how to do just that.

Once you have the basic blueprint down for improving your mental game, you need a way to objectively measure your progress. In Chapter 5, I'll tell you about the diagnostic routine I put myself through at the end of every season I played, and how pushing your ego aside will supercharge your rate of improvement.

When you talk about the "soft" skills that make up the mental part of golf, you first have to overcome the natural skepticism that people have. It's easy for an amateur player to say, "That's fine for a tour player, who hits the ball great. What about me?" But the reality is that tour players struggle with factors like confidence, focus, and self-belief all the time, just like amateur players. The great news is that any player—whether you're a 30-handicapper or Rory McIlroy—can learn those arts. There's a process you can follow to improve your self-belief and play with confidence—and rescue yourself if you start to slip during a round. We'll talk about it in Chapter 6.

If you think about the course you know and love the best, what separates it from the others? Part of it is probably the way it suits your eye. Another is familiarity. You know the holes and the best way to play them with the game you have. There's no substitute for familiarity, but you can adapt the same principles and feelings you get at your favorite course to play any course better. In Chapter 7, I'll show you how to better judge risk and reward and play smarter—a skill that shows up no matter how well you're swinging on a particular day.

Chapters 8 and 9 are two of my favorite subjects to talk

about when it comes to growing and enjoying the game. Playing a casual weekend round with your buddies might be a way to blow off steam, but business golf is a different thing entirely. In Chapter 8, I'll show you how to calm your nerves, make conversation, and stay competitive during your round with bosses, clients or co-workers. If you have kids, family, or friends that you'd like to introduce to the game, Chapter 9 will show you how to offer encouragement and guidance without overwhelming a new player with information, however well meaning.

My goal for you is to get through the first couple of chapters in this book and see that your best golf isn't as far away as you may have thought. With some basic mental training, you're going to change the way you think about your game, and you're going to change your scores.

I think you'll like what you find.

1
INSIDE THE ROPES

WATCHING a tour player hit balls on the range can almost put you in a trance. It still happens to me, and I've been watching it—or doing it myself—for more than fifty years.

There's no question that players at the highest levels of the game have some incredible physical talents. You need strength, speed, and coordination to make the golf ball do what you want it to do, time after time. When you think about how fast the clubhead is moving, and how precisely it needs to meet the ground and the back of the ball on a full shot, it's truly amazing what even a run-of-the-mill tour player can do.

I'm not bringing this up to try to discourage you, or to make this game seem impossible.

In fact, it's the opposite.

Just think about that long line of players at the range on a Wednesday before a tour event. To a person, they all look like they're never going to miss. Every one of them has been the best player in the field at a given tournament—whether it's junior golf, high school, college, or on one of the professional tours.

And yet most of those players go out and hit all kinds of strange shots come tournament time. They hit a hook the one time they can't afford to miss left, or they leave it short in the one bunker that's just dead. Or maybe they're just a few percentage points less sharp than they were on the range.

What separates the average player on one of the professional tours from Jack Nicklaus or Tiger Woods or Annika Sorenstam? When you look at the records of the players who really thrived in the most pressure-packed circumstances, did those results come because players like Jack, Tiger, or Annika could do things physically that other players couldn't? Did they have swings that were so much more technically superior than everyone else's?

Or is it because they mastered the game's mental side?

I played head-to-head with Jack Nicklaus in college and as a tour player for forty years. And I've worked with dozens of tour players who have teed up next to Tiger Woods and Annika Sorenstam for the last twenty years.

I believe that the players who separate themselves from the rest of the pack do it with the mind, not with muscle or the quality of their swing. Look at the mental change that Phil Mickelson went through before the 2013 British Open. He totally changed the way he saw shots he needed to hit and went out and won a tournament that nobody believed he could. He pictured the shots he needed on a links course and practiced those shots. Afterward, he said it was the most rewarding win of his career.

Does it help to be able to carry the ball 290 yards like Jack could in the 1960s, when we were all thrilled with a 250-yard tee shot? Absolutely. But Tom Weiskopf and Johnny Miller could do everything Jack could do physically, and they didn't combine to have careers as good as Jack's worst decade on the PGA Tour. Can Tiger do things with the golf ball that Jack never dreamed possible? Absolutely. But the tour is filled with physical powerhouses who can do the same things—players like Phil Mickelson, Ernie Els and Adam Scott. The same was true for Annika Sorenstam when she raised her game in the last ten years of her career. She dominated the LPGA like few have in the history of the women's game, but she wasn't doing anything physically different than Karrie Webb or Se Ri Pak.

Tour players as a group have access to the best physical training, coaching, clubfitting, caddying and all-around golf expertise that money can buy. Heck, there are so many experts trying to get involved in the game that a prominent tour player could build an all-star team that would work for free.

With all of that knowledge available to them, why is it that so many players concentrate such a large percentage of their time on the part of the game that *doesn't* have the most impact on their performance?

Many tour players will spend 90 percent of their time working on the physical mechanics of the swing, when the mental component of the game—handling emotions, making decisions, playing through adversity, following a routine—makes up a good 90 percent of their results.

Why is that? And what does it have to do with you and your game?

I'll tell you.

When you have tremendous physical talent, it's seductive to hear an "expert" give you a list of four or five things you can do to make a "perfect" swing. Then, all a tour player has to do is flick the switch on the computer and go out and make sixty-seven or sixty-eight perfect swings, right?

And when the "perfect" swing fails during a crucial moment, it's easier for the tour player to handle the failure by telling himself that he just needs to hit more balls to fix some perceived mechanical flaw so he can do better the next time.

The truth is, there's no such thing as perfect. And you don't need to be anywhere near perfect to get the most out of your ability.

I know it firsthand, because I did it for fifty years.

I was *never* the most dominant player in my group. I didn't have much of an amateur career before college, because my dad made me work in the summers so I'd have more of an appreciation for the game. At USC, I had a nice career and won some tournaments, including the Pac-10 individual title, and I made it to the quarterfinals of the 1963 U.S. Amateur. But I wasn't Nicklaus by any stretch of the imagination. In the NCAA Tournament in 1961, our fifth man had Jack 2-down on the fifth hole. Jack told his coach to come pick him up on the 14th green because the match was going to be over.

It was. Nicklaus beat him 5 and 4. And the next year, Jack won the first of his eighteen major championships at Oakmont, in a playoff over Arnold Palmer.

I turned pro in 1964, and when I got out for my first extended look at tour golf, I could immediately see that guys like Jack—and even guys like Ron Gillespie and Jim McPhate, who came out from my hometown the same time I did and were also taught by my father—were way better ballstrikers than I would ever be.

I knew I needed to come up with a different strategy to stay out there.

By developing the ability to control my emotions, stay in my comfort zone and never give up on the course—skills I first learned from my dad—I had a very successful career. I won at Colonial in 1967, my third year out, and nine other times on the regular tour—including the 1970 and 1976 PGA Championships. I won fourteen more tournaments—including three majors—on the Champions Tour.

My record certainly isn't as flashy as Jack's, or Gary Player's or Lee Trevino's. But I'm proud of the fact that I rarely gave tournaments away when I was in position to win. The moment usually didn't get too big for me—but it didn't seem to happen enough for my liking!

You may have already heard my story about starting my week at the 1970 PGA at Southern Hills visualizing myself walking up to the 18th green on Sunday with the crowd cheering me on—and having it turn out exactly the way I pictured it. I got the idea from reading Maxwell Maltz's book *Psycho-Cybernetics,* which we'll talk about more in Chapter 6.

Another great example of the power of visualization and self-talk comes from a tournament I didn't win—the 1974 Masters.

One of the only regrets I have in my career is that I never won the Masters. I would give almost anything to slip on that green jacket knowing I was going to be in that special group of champions. You'd get to go to the dinner and listen to stories from Sam Snead, Byron Nelson, and Ben Hogan, and you could come back forever—or at least as long as you could reach the par-4s in two shots!

The closest I ever came was in 1974. I went into the pressroom on Saturday night with a two-shot lead. The greens had been really slow, and I decided I was going to put some lead tape on my Ray Cook putter for the next day. But I got caught up talking to the media until late, and it got dark. I didn't have a chance to go out and practice after the press conferences. I forgot to add the tape, and the next day I took nineteen putts on the front nine. On No. 13, I hit driver, 4-iron to about 15 feet, and I left my eagle putt an inch short—something I never, ever do. To this day I feel like I lost the Masters by one strip of lead tape.

Gary Player was paired with me, and I watched him extricate himself from trouble time and time again. On 13, he hit a persimmon wood from out of the trees, 240 yards out, and bounced it in front of the creek. It bounced on the bridge and bounced into the bunker. He blasted it out to just in front of me. After he watched my eagle putt roll up there, just short, he put his into the middle of the cup for birdie.

He shot 70 to my 73 and ended up beating me and Tom

Weiskopf by two shots. I'll never forget what he said afterward—"I knew I was going to win on the first tee." That's an amazing thing for a player to say out loud, but it shouldn't surprise anybody who knows Gary Player. He got every ounce out of his ability—both by keeping himself in phenomenal shape and by willing himself to reach his goals with one of the strongest minds in the game. How else can you explain a five-foot-seven, 150-pound man who hit it 40 yards behind Nicklaus having Gary's record? The same is true for my friend Lee Trevino, who used his own mental strength—not a textbook swing—to face Nicklaus down in Jack's absolute prime at both the 1971 U.S. Open and 1972 British Open.

The reality of tour life is that for the most part, you're out there on your own, trying to figure things out as you go along. The financial stakes were different when I came out on tour—$10,000 was a lot of money then—but the pressures were the same. You're out there trying to make a living week in and week out, and you have to prove yourself over and over again.

It takes a special kind of self-confidence just to get to the tour in the first place. The odds are so stacked against anybody—and the field of players so good—that you have to have a certain amount of self-belief to simply tee your ball for the first time as an exempt player. But it's a testament to how stressful and challenging professional golf is that every player—from Jack Nicklaus down to the guy you've never heard of—goes through a crisis of confidence from time to time.

The difference is, the best players know how to get that confidence back—either through their own processes, or by trusting the right group of people to help. I was fortunate to have my dad as my coach for the majority of my career on the regular tour, and then to have my son Ron coach me from 1987 on through my senior career. They not only knew me and my game and offered an extra set of eyes, but they also gave me the knowledge and confidence to make mental and physical adjustments on my own when I was out on the course. The best teachers and advisors do that—they give the player that confidence so that they never feel helpless, even during the most stressful times.

I don't think I ever stood on the first tee of a tournament round feeling like I had no chance for something good to happen that day. That doesn't mean I always shot a great score. But I never felt like I was going through the motions. I was free to concentrate on competing and making the most of what I had. One of the most phenomenal things I've ever heard of is Tiger Woods making 142 cuts in a row. He might have had bad days, but he always overcame them.

Professional golf is fascinating in that the vast majority of tournament play is individual. You're out there getting judged by the shots you hit and the scores you post. But some of the most pressure-packed golf any player will ever face comes in an almost completely alien format—at the Ryder Cup. To start with, the guys on each team are playing for something much bigger than themselves or prize money— they're representing their country. Add in the fact that most of the week is spent playing alternate shot or better ball—

formats tour players almost never play—and the stress level can be off the charts. I'll never forget standing next to Billy Casper and his wife Shirley during the opening ceremonies of my first Ryder Cup as a player, in 1971. They were raising the American flag, and tears were streaming down both of their faces. It's safe to say that's something you didn't see when Billy was standing on the first tee at a Masters or a U.S. Open.

That year, the matches were at Old Warson, in St. Louis. Jay Hebert was the captain, and he showed a lot of favoritism toward the older players on the team—guys he had played with, like Gene Littler and Miller Barber. I was playing so well coming in, and on the first day Jay paired me with Jack Nicklaus for alternate shot. Jack and I don't exactly play the same kind of game, and both of us spent the morning hitting shots we weren't used to seeing. Tony Jacklin and Brian Huggett handled us, 3 and 2.

After that, he sat me for the afternoon and the next day, too. I was going berserk because I was playing the best golf of my life and I wasn't out there. By the time we got to singles, I was a little stale. I halved my morning match against Bernard Gallacher, and won 1-up in the afternoon over Peter Townsend. We ended up winning the cup 18.5 to 13.5, but I felt like it was in spite of Hebert, not because of him. It also helped to have Nicklaus, Palmer, Trevino, and Snead on your side.

My second experience as a player in the Ryder Cup, at Royal Lytham & St. Annes, England, in 1977, was totally different. Dow Finsterwald was captain, and the way he handled the team inspired a good bit of what I would eventually do as captain of the 1991 team.

I came to Lytham playing completely the opposite of the way I was in 1970. I couldn't find it. Finsterwald put me out there with Jerry McGee on the first morning for alternate shot against Neil Coles and Peter Dawson, and Jerry was just the perfect partner. We hit the ball pretty much the same length, so we had the same kinds of clubs into greens. And Jerry was calm and consistent. I was spraying the ball all over the place and putting Jerry in terrible positions. We were wearing the polyester pants that were popular at the time, and by the back nine, Jerry had been in the bushes trying to play my shots out of there so often that he looked like he had been attacked by a cat, with threads hanging out everywhere. I hit what felt like my first good shot of the day on 16—a tee shot that trickled into the first cut of thin rough. I told Jerry to just get it up there on the green somewhere with an 8-iron, and he knocked it to about 30 feet. I made that putt, which left us 1-down with two to go. On 17, Jerry drove it dead straight and perfect. Unfortunately, there was a bunker in the middle of the fairway. I couldn't do anything but pitch out sideways, and we were still short of where the other guys were. Jerry had 6-iron into the green, and I told him the same thing—just get it on the green. He hit a good shot, but it released to the back fringe, leaving me with about a 50-footer. Neil and Peter had about 25 feet for birdie. I made my putt, and they three putted, so the match was all square. On 18, I hit my first fairway of the day, and Neil and Peter put it in the bunker and never finished the hole. We won 1-up.

The same pattern held on Friday for better ball. Dave Hill played great, and carried me the whole way in our 5-

and-3 win over Tony Jacklin and Eamonn Darcy. I sat for the singles, and the U.S. won the cup 12.5 to 7.5.

Those 1977 matches were the last ones before Seve Ballesteros showed up for Europe. He almost single-handedly saved the Ryder Cup and made it the relevant and important event it is today. He was such a force in the game by 1979 that Great Britain's team was expanded to include the rest of Europe so he could play—and make the matches an actual contest. The U.S. hadn't lost the cup since 1957, and the event had become pretty much a parade lap for the Americans by the 1970s.

But Seve was something else entirely. He thrived on the team aspect of the competition, and his intensity often carried the entire European team—no matter whether Seve was actually playing well or not. People always ask me what was the best Ryder Cup pairing I ever saw, and I'd have to say it was Seve and anybody they put him with. By himself, he was such an intimidating factor, and he was never out of a hole. Put him with a partner to feed off of and he was almost unbeatable. He and José Maria Olazábal played together fifteen times and lost twice.

It's also important to mention how much Tony Jacklin had to do with building a strong European side. Guys like Seve hit the shots, but when Tony became captain of the European Team for the first time in 1983, he insisted that things be done in a first-class way for his players, like we were doing it over here. He wanted his players to believe that they were every bit as talented and accomplished as the Americans, and his confidence in them rubbed off in how they played.

Thanks to Jacklin's trailblazing and the addition of players like Seve, Olazábal and Bernhard Langer, I knew I was going to have a fight on my hands when I was named captain for the 1991 matches at Kiawah Island. The European Team had taken the cup at the last three meetings—keeping it in 1989 because of a tie score. I figured it was time to try something different.

From the time I was named captain, in late 1989, I was determined to do everything I could to promote the matches and prepare myself to lead the best team we could possibly have. Instead of working on my own game—I would become eligible for the Champions Tour in November 1991, right after the Ryder Cup—or doing corporate outings, I spent most of my time the second half of the 1990 PGA Tour season and two thirds of the 1991 season out on the PGA Tour, getting a feel for the players who had a chance to make the team.

The PGA Tour was great about giving me some control over some of the Tuesday shoot-out pairings and formats early in the season, so I paired different players together to see how they worked with each other. From my own experience playing in two Ryder Cups, I knew how important it was for players to play with partners who allowed them the best chance to play at their optimum comfort level. I sent guys like Corey Pavin, Paul Azinger, Hale Irwin, Mark Calcavecchia, Lanny Wadkins and Payne Stewart out in various configurations to see how they handled alternate shot together, and to get feedback from the players themselves about potential pairings they liked and didn't like.

When it came time to make the captain's choices, the

way different players were playing was certainly a factor, but the partnership, leadership, and personality aspect of the two guys who would be added to the team were much more important to me. I asked some of the key guys on my team who I knew would be in the mix—Paul Azinger, Payne Stewart, Lanny Wadkins, Hale Irwin—who they wanted to play with. Raymond Floyd was an automatic choice. My plan was to have Raymond paired with Fred Couples and be his backbone for the week. The other choice was harder. I had three people in mind—Chip Beck, Tom Watson, and Tom Kite. I went with Chip because of his attitude, and the fact that he made a good pairing with Paul Azinger. John Daly had just won the PGA, and there was a lot of fan speculation about me picking him, but I didn't know much about him at that point, and I wanted to build a team that had a strong mental makeup. John has some incredible skills, but I don't think that team play would be his strongest suit.

After I had my team, I had each of the guys complete a specialized questionnaire developed by Dr. Deborah Graham, a terrific golf psychologist based in Texas. Her test helps people see what personality type they really have and the kinds of players that make the most compatible match. It's hard to summarize her test in a few words, but it basically uncovered your baseline competitive traits: Are you more of a creative person, or are you more technical? Do you compete at a fast pace, or a slow one? What kind of competitive arousal level do you have? Do you get angry when you play, and does that anger help or hurt you? Or do you not get angry enough?

I took the test myself first, to evaluate it, and it showed

me things about myself and my game that were not only incredibly insightful and accurate, but a huge help when I eventually got out on the Champions Tour full time in 1992. I learned that I was a hugely aggressive player—stupidly aggressive, considering how short I hit the ball—and that my willingness to interact with other players and fans out on the course could be hurting my concentration. It just blew me away. By combining the results of the test and the feedback I got from seeing the different guys play together over the previous year, I had a great road map showing how and what the different players were thinking and feeling, and a preview of how they would respond to each other.

When we got to Kiawah Island, it wasn't the time for me to dump a huge amount of information on the players and try to coach them in any way about their swings. My job was to get out of the way and put them in the best position to win. Floyd and Fred Couples were a terrific match—Raymond's steadiness and incredible short game freed Freddie up to play the way he loves to play—loose and long. They went 2-1 in three matches together.

When the American team struggles—particularly high-profile guys like Tiger Woods or Phil Mickelson—you hear people wonder why it should matter who a guy's partner is. If you're Tiger Woods, the thinking goes, you should be able to play with a guy off the street and win a match.

But Ryder Cup golf is totally different than regular golf. It's a different animal. When you hit a bad shot out on the tour, you get a chance to go out and rectify it yourself—and if you don't, you're the only one responsible. In the Ryder

Cup, you feel like you want to apologize to your partner when you hit a bad shot, and that's awkward to do with somebody you spend every other week of the year trying to beat. Golf is a hard game, and it takes a lot just to be able to take care of yourself, never mind carry around somebody else.

And the simple fact is that a player can be as talented and patriotic as humanly possible, but if you put him with somebody he isn't comfortable with, no amount of individual heroics is usually enough to offset that—especially when you're playing against pairings like Seve Ballesteros and José Maria Olazábal. Those guys could come into the Ryder Cup having missed their last ten cuts each, but when they played together, they believed they couldn't be beaten. And they were almost always right.

Paul Azinger, the captain of the 2008 team that won the cup at Valhalla, came up with the neatest idea to help put them in the best position to play well. He picked three assistants to help him—me, Ray Floyd, and Olin Browne, and he put each one of us in charge of one of three "pods" of players with similar personalities and complementary styles—based on some of the techniques that the Navy SEALs use to build teams. The players in each pod practiced together, and they were ready to be paired in basically any configuration within that group of four. My guys—Chad Campbell, Stewart Cink, Ben Curtis and Steve Stricker—were all calm, steady players. Every guy knew what to expect in terms of pairings during the event, and they were all comfortable with their roles. Paul's book on that process—called *Cracking the Code*—is a fascinating read, even for somebody who was in the team room, like I was. It was a brilliant strategy.

Does that mean they weren't nervous, or that they didn't hit bad shots? No. But it freed them from a lot of the stress and uncertainty that comes with Ryder Cup play. They played great golf, and beat the highly favored Europeans 16.5 to 11.5.

If you need any more proof that golf is mostly mental, just look at the example of Tiger Woods in the Ryder Cup. Tiger has been the undisputed best player in the game since 1997. He's generally acknowledged to be the toughest competitor on the PGA Tour—mentally tough, brutally intimidating, and seemingly immune to major championship pressure.

But when Tiger gets to the Ryder Cup, his record is pretty ordinary. He's 4-1-2 in singles, but 9-16-1 when he plays with a partner. He's actually lost more team matches than any player in U.S. Ryder Cup history. Part of that, of course, is the fact that he plays almost every match. But when you compare Tiger's record to the previous generation of superstars—Jack Nicklaus, Arnold Palmer, Lee Trevino, and Billy Casper—he doesn't match up.

Why?

I think part of it is that Tiger doesn't put the same value on the Ryder Cup that he does major championships. He seems to get into the events and mix very well with the other players, but I don't think he burns to win the Cup the way that players like Seve, Peter Oosterhuis or Ian Poulter have for Europe, or Larry Nelson did for the United States. Payne Stewart, Lanny Wadkins, Paul Azinger, and I spent many, many hours together throughout the 1991 season just talking Ryder Cup strategy. We lived it. I don't know that Tiger will ever live the Ryder Cup like he does the Masters or the U.S. Open.

But I believe a bigger part of it is that he isn't always in a pairing that brings out the best in him. Tiger is usually paired with guys he personally likes—Steve Stricker, Jim Furyk—instead of guys he could mentor. When you think back to the 2012 Ryder Cup, the biggest story early in the week was Keegan Bradley, and how he flourished with a veteran Phil Mickelson as his partner. Tiger would be terrific in that role, but he doesn't usually get the chance. I don't care how many major championships you've won. It's damn hard to win a match in the Ryder Cup if you aren't bringing the best out of your partner, and vice versa.

To Hal Sutton's credit, he tried to do just that at Oakland Hills in 2004. After the experiment of putting Tiger and Phil together twice on the first day turned out to be a disaster, Sutton sent Tiger and Chris Riley out Friday morning for a four-ball match against Darren Clarke and Ian Poulter. Chris's job was to go out there and hit some greens and challenge Tiger to hit it inside him. Tiger took to it, and they played great as a team—winning 4 and 3. The problem was that Riley had never even played a practice round with Tiger before that. The experience of playing with the best player in the world—and all the attention that comes with it—just exhausted him. Sutton wanted to send them out again in the afternoon, but Riley begged off. Tiger went out with Davis Love, and they got beat 4 and 3 in foursomes by Padraig Harrington and Paul McGinley.

This is a guy who decided he was going to win the U.S. Open on a broken leg, and who went out and proceeded not just to do it, but to walk an entire extra round and win an 18-hole playoff. How could that guy be the same one who went 0-3-1 at Medinah in 2012?

It's not how you hit the shots. It's how you use your mind to picture them.

2
WHY TRYING DOESN'T WORK

IT doesn't matter if I'm teaching Rory McIlroy, Phil Mickelson, or a 20-handicap executive at a one-day clinic. My goal is always the same: to get players to think more clearly and simply, and to use the skills they already have to improve their game.

That might sound *too* simple, especially if you're used to hearing a hundred different mechanical thoughts and swing theories from a teacher.

But the reality is that most people struggle because they get out onto the course and do things that make the game much harder than it needs to be. Some of the instincts that have been drummed into you since you were a kid—like being very careful and taking your time when completing an important task—are just about the worst things that can happen to your golf swing.

Let me give you an example.

Tour players hit thousands and thousands of balls over the course of a season. Most of these shots come on the practice range, and a bunch more of them happen during practice rounds. Other ones come when a player doesn't have a real chance to win a tournament. For even the best players, a tiny percentage of shots actually happen under maximum pressure—to win a tournament, make a cut, qualify for a tour card, or some other super-important consequence.

If you had to guess, do you think a player would have a better chance of hitting a good shot by approaching it as if it was just like any other shot, or by approaching it like it was the most important shot in the world?

I hope you guessed the first answer—because if you can accept that and incorporate it even a little bit into your game, you're going to play the best you've ever played.

You've seen it happen a million times on the professional tours. A player comes out and plays great for a couple of days, and is either in contention or has the outright lead on Sunday. Then, as the holes click by on Sunday afternoon, his or her pattern starts to change. More time gets spent on reading greens. You see more practice swings. You see a slower—or a faster—pre-shot routine.

Everything that player is doing is sabotaging his or her best chance to hit good shots. He or she is transferring the golf swing from the subconscious mind to the conscious mind. Instead of just doing something that is basically automatic—at least for a tour player—he or she starts trying to control all of the complicated movement and timing that goes into a golf swing. And it's just impossible to do that consistently well, even in the lowest-pressure situations.

Traditionally, a handicap in golf is the number that approximates your scoring potential. But the real golf handicap is the one players put on themselves by *trying* to make a perfect swing instead of *seeing* the shot they want to hit and feeling the swing they have to make to create it.

I've talked about it before, but it's worth mentioning again—in fact, it's so valuable that I start off every first lesson I give with it. If I asked you to sign your name on your scorecard, you'd do it in a second, without any extra thinking. You've been signing your name for years, and it probably comes out pretty much the same each time. But if I asked you to go back and duplicate the signature you just made, and I asked you to take your time doing it, it would take you much longer, and it wouldn't have nearly the same flow to it. It'd be uncomfortable.

This proves that the subconscious mind is where you want to be.

I'm not saying that there's no place for trying to copy somebody else's swing, or for making mechanical improvements. A good teacher knows how to deliver that information and help you work on it on the practice tee. I'm just saying that the time to *try* to move that club through the swing isn't when you're out on the 16th tee during the first match of your club championship.

When I talk about this with some of the tour players I teach, I get some interesting responses at first. One player said he slowed things down under the gun because he wanted to make sure he made all of his reads and was as ready and calm as he could be for an important shot.

I can understand that kind of thinking. After all, how many times did your parents tell you to be careful and take your time when doing something complicated? But for most shots—especially on or around the greens—that doesn't work very well.

If you normally take sixty seconds to read a putt and another fifteen seconds to go through your pre-putt routine over the ball, any extra time you add to that process to do something you don't normally do—like make a second read, or make an extra practice stroke over the ball—hurts you in a lot of ways. First, the extra time gives you more time to let the pressure of the moment build. Extra time doesn't calm you down. It produces *more* stress.

Second, surveying a putt (or a full shot) from extra angles that you don't normally see introduces the potential for more doubt. You're spending more time standing over a read trying to figure out if the break is six inches or eight inches outside left, and then standing over the ball wondering if you made the right decision. Reading the putt the same way you always do and rolling it with confidence will produce far, far better results over time.

I played my entire career with that mind-set, but it's an attitude that is applicable to any player. I was lucky enough to be paired with my good friend Al Geiberger in 1977 when he shot the first 59 in PGA Tour history, in the second round of the Danny Thomas Memphis Classic at Colonial Country Club in Cordova, Tennessee. I can tell you that shooting that kind of score that day, on that golf course, was just incredible. The course was in terrible shape, and it played long and difficult. Even though we were playing lift, clean and place, the greens were very grainy, and it was hard to make *any* putt.

We started our round on the 10th hole, and Al birdied two out of the first five holes—a nice start, but nothing crazy. He was really rolling the ball great on the greens, and I was struggling with my putter—two things that didn't happen very often. As Jerry McGee and I stood to the side of the first green—our 10th hole, a long par-5—we chatted a bit. Jerry said that up to that point, Al had been closest to the pin only twice out of the ten holes but was already 6-under, while Jerry was 2-under and I was 2-over. As we were talking, Al proceeded to hole his chip to go 8-under after 10.

That's when we knew something special could be happening.

Al and I have been great friends for years—he got out of USC just before I got there—and we had played a ton of golf together on tour up to that point. Our normal routine was to have plenty of conversation during our tournament rounds together—talking about where we were going to room together next, or how he was dealing with some of the physical ailments he had. I didn't want to get in Al's way during this special round, but I knew that I had to treat him the same way I usually did. That way, I wouldn't get him thinking about where he stood simply because things had gotten weird and quiet with his playing partners. So I did my best to make him feel like it was a ho-hum day—even when he birdied 15 and 16 to get to 12-under.

I can tell you that Al stayed exactly the same throughout that round—the same way he had been in the dozens of other rounds we had played together. He was just in that zone where he was swinging great, keeping it simple, and not letting his emotions overtake him. The thing about Al is that he makes it look so easy all the time, with that great swing and that good, sound game. But on this day, there wasn't a single shot that was shaky, from the tee to the hole. He kept his foot on the accelerator the entire time, and the putt he made on 18 went right into the heart. There was never a doubt.

I've asked Al many times in the years since if he was aware of what kind of round was unfolding there. He says he wasn't. I know he asked his caddie, Lee Lynch, for a new ball every few holes, and he didn't notice that the guy handed him the exact same ball every time. So I'd say he was pretty focused on the picture in his head of what he wanted to do— and not the consequences of making a bad swing.

Other guys have shot 59 on tour since then, but I don't think anybody has done anything close to what Al accomplished that day. That course was the least likely place in the entire world for somebody to set that record. The only thing I can think of that's in the same league is the 59 that David Duval shot on the Palmer Course in the final round of the 1999 Bob Hope. That's the toughest of the courses they play out there, but the greens are just pure. Still, to eagle the final hole to shoot 59 and win by a shot is amazing in its own right.

Another great example of this concept comes from a conversation I had with Byron Nelson over lunch at the 1974 Masters. I asked him if he had any swing thoughts he used during that incredible streak of eleven tournament wins in a row in 1945. He smiled and said something that astonished me, but at the same time made a lot of sense.

Before the West Coast swing early that season, he found a swing thought that really worked for him. He never told me what the thought was, but that's not important. What's important is that for the rest of the year, he followed the same routine: He would go to the range about thirty minutes before his tee time just to warm up his muscles, and then he'd go play using only that one swing thought. He played thirty-five events that season and won eighteen of them—including those eleven in a row. As the season progressed, he didn't practice more, or spend more time warming up before his rounds. He did everything the same—and he didn't do anything that got in the way of a simple, clearheaded approach. It was as simple as using one swing thought for the whole year.

It was a great learning experience for me. I had come into the week thinking seven or eight different things about my own swing, and that conversation showed me how simple it could be. It clicked, and I went out and had my best finish at the Masters, a tie for second behind Gary Player.

I'm using these dramatic examples to illustrate a fundamental problem many players have, even at the tour level. They operate under the assumption that some information is good, so more must be better. Or that hitting a small bucket of balls is useful, so hitting a large one must be better. Tour players will call and tell Ronnie, Junior, or myself that they want to book three consecutive days with us out in California, so they can really immerse themselves in what we're teaching.

But they really need to do the opposite.

When I see a tour player, two hours is about the maximum amount of time we need to be together. That works out to thirty or forty-five minutes for putting, thirty or forty-five minutes for short game, and thirty or forty-five minutes just chatting about many of the mental concepts we're going to discuss in the next few chapters. After that, I want the player to go away and play for a few weeks with the one or two simple things I left him with. Then, if he needs a refresher or a tune-up later on, we can meet up again. I want them to be able to resist the temptation to gorge themselves on the new information, overexaggerate it and grind all of the feel out of it over five hundred practice putts. Part of my dad's genius as an instructor was understanding how to help players improve without overwhelming them with more than they needed—or could handle—and I like to think that my sons and I have followed that tradition.

The world of golf instruction is where this whole concept of "trying" got tied up with the misconception that a golf swing is something you can actually fully direct with your conscious mind. A player spends his or her entire golfing life swinging the club with a certain pattern, and then when he or she faces an "important" shot, he or she thinks he can all of a sudden take conscious control of the legs, torso, arms, and hands and make an effective swing.

Like I said, I can understand why players get pulled down that road. It happened to me the week I won my first tour event, at Colonial in 1967. I went out and shot 65-66 the first two days to take a big lead and break Ben Hogan's 36-hole tournament scoring record by four shots. It was about as good as I could play. Then, in the third round, I was paired with Gardner Dickinson—who slow-played me and did everything he could think of to get me off my game. It worked on this raw twenty-six-year-old, and my approach totally changed. I started second-guessing myself and taking more time over all of my shots—and getting progressively more disgusted with myself for giving so many shots back. I coughed up the entire lead to go into Sunday tied with Tom Weiskopf.

Back in the locker room, I was sitting by my locker completely dejected, and I heard a voice asking where Dave Stockton's locker was. Then Hogan himself walked around the corner and shook my hand. He told me that he didn't say anything to me the day before because I didn't need any more back-slapping, but that now that I had my bad round out of the way I had a great chance to go out and win. It was so cool for him to be so encouraging—especially when he was in contention as well. I went out and did just that the next day, and won by two shots—and it changed my career.

It's really up to you. You can go to the range every day, get a dozen lessons and hit five hundred balls in an attempt to build the "muscle memory" of a so-called perfect swing—which doesn't really exist. Or, you can change the way you think about the game and see the shot you want to hit, so that you can play your best golf no matter what kind of swing you have that day—or that year.

Once you can disconnect from the obsession with me-chanics and start thinking about and seeing your actual shots, you're going to be amazed at what happens. When we host clinics with a dozen average amateur players, it doesn't take more than ten minutes before the first "I can't believe it's this easy" comment pops up. Or an otherwise good player who is struggling with his or her stroke says something like, "This feels so good. It's how I used to do it."

I want you to think way, way less about *how* you do it, and way, way more about *what* you're going to do.

Remember, trying harder isn't the solution. Thinking better is.

3

HOW TO PLAY
UNDER PRESSURE

GOLF is pretty much defined by pressure.

It's the main reason the swings you make on the range are hard to take to the golf course.

The ones on the course have consequences.

I'm not just talking about big, obvious pressure, like what you get coming down the stretch at a major championship. There doesn't have to be millions of people watching, a chance to make history, or millions of dollars at stake to push the needle to an uncomfortable place. It's all relative.

If your tendency is to lose shots to the right, you're going to feel it when you get to the tee and see trouble all down the right side. If you've never broken 90 (or 80 or 70), you're going to feel it when you have a chance to make that milestone on the last few holes.

You're going to experience it when you have a bad hole and you're on the next tee, mad at yourself for what just happened. Will you be able to clear that from your mind and get back on track, or will you compound your bad score and get completely derailed?

Walk down the practice range at your course and watch different players hitting balls. You don't need a trained eye to quickly get a sense for which players hit the ball great and which ones don't hit it quite so good.

But the difference in physical skill isn't what produces the most separation between the guys playing in the championship flight and the ones playing in the B or C flight.

It's mind-set.

It's how you handle the big and small pressures that come with every hole you play. It's how well you keep your composure when things get difficult, and whether or not you continue to make solid decisions based on a rational assessment of your own game.

Very, very few people hit the ball flawlessly—even at the tour level. It would obviously be nice to have a classically ideal swing like Adam Scott's or Suzann Pettersen's, but that's just not a realistic goal.

But that's no reason to get discouraged. The biggest strides you're going to take as a golfer aren't going to come by trying to make your swing more like Adam's or Suzann's. They're going to come by improving how you handle competitive pressure—which we're going to talk about here— and your course management decisions. We'll get to that in Chapter 7.

So how do you get the best out of yourself? By building a routine you can follow no matter what the circumstances are.

When I use the term "routine," it probably triggers some thoughts for you. If you watch tournament golf, you've certainly heard the commentators talk about a player's pre-shot routine. They're usually referring to the set of physical motions a player goes through that lead up to the act of pulling the club back.

But a complete routine is more than just a collection of physical moves you repeat in the fifteen or twenty seconds before you swing. It's much more. A true routine starts much earlier than those last few seconds before the swing starts. It incorporates your reaction to the previous shot you hit, and it lasts through the next shot you hit. So many bad rounds happen because a single mental mistake produces a bad shot, and that bad shot snowballs into a mental meltdown and a series of big numbers on the card.

What makes up a good routine? To me, it has three important things. It's based on your personal speed. It's something that's comfortable for you to follow. And it ends with a positive image of the shot you're about to hit.

Personal speed is a subjective thing, but I suspect you already have a good idea if you are a "fast" or "slow" person. If you walk fast, talk fast, and get impatient quickly, you're obviously a fast person—and a fast person needs a brisk routine. If you take things at a more leisurely pace, you're obviously going to do better with a more deliberate routine.

Since a routine—by definition—is something that you do for every shot, it makes sense to have one that is comfortable for you. Camilo Villegas's putting routine includes a Spider-Man-like move where he gets down close to the ground to see his line. That's not going to work for everybody. Just because Tiger Woods—or me, or any other tour player—does a certain thing in his or her routine doesn't mean that it's going to work for you.

What your routine *does* need to work well is comfort, consistency, and a good ending. And by good ending I mean that it leaves you with a positive image of the shot you want to hit (or putt you want to roll) right before you pull the trigger. My son Ronnie knows my putting stroke better than anybody in the world. And for years, he tried to copy it to improve his own putting. He had some success, but his results really jumped when he started copying my routine—which happened to suit him because he's a fast person, like I am—instead of my stroke. My mental and physical routine is dominated by picturing the exact shot I'm about to hit, and I rely on it to keep me even and positive throughout the round. That's the part that clicked for Ronnie—and most of the other players we teach—not a mechanical tweak.

We see so many players with terrible routines, even at the tour level. They go through an entire round where they don't make a thing, then come to the practice green, drop a couple of balls and immediately roll them in. They wonder why it happens that way, and we explain that it's because on the practice green, they didn't go through this whole pre-shot procedure that not only wasn't helping, but actually hurt their results.

Once you build a routine that is consistent with your

speed, is comfortable, and incorporates actually seeing the shot you want to hit before you hit it, you'll be able to practice with it before you play, then simply repeat the same pattern when you go out and play for real.

I want to emphasize again that it's important for you to build a routine that suits your personality and is comfortable for you to do. A routine that doesn't fit is not only going to be hard for you to follow, it's not going to help you much either. The whole goal is to get yourself focused on seeing your shot and immersed in your routine, so that you can relax.

That said, I want to give you a description of my routine for a series of shots on a hole you recognize—the par-3 12th at Augusta—so you can get a sense for what a good routine does and doesn't do.

A good routine has two distinct pieces. The first piece covers the time from your last shot until you start the process of hitting the next shot, and the second piece is your actual mental and physical pre-shot routine for the shot at hand.

After I've putted out on the 11th green at Augusta, I turn and look at the tops of the trees near the 12th tee to get a general idea of what the wind is doing. By the time you actually get to the 12th tee, you can't feel any wind because you're blocked by the trees and the grandstand, so it's critical to start picking up information as soon as possible.

Once I get to the tee, my first move is to determine the yardage to the flag and pick the two best clubs for the shot. I take both of these clubs with me to the back of the tee and check out what the flag and trees are doing down by the green. (This is where a lot of amateur players get in trouble.

They read the yardage in the cart, pick one club, and go up on the tee—but if they see that they might need more or less club, they're usually too lazy to go back and change. They're never fully committed to the club they have in their hands. We'll talk more about this in Chapter 7.) Depending on where the flag is—a few steps beyond the water in front, or in back, just in front of the bunker—I'll make my club selection. The location of the flag to the left or right of the green will also help determine which side of the box I pick to tee up my ball. I like to play shots right to left, and by moving to the left side of the tee box, I can totally change the look of the shot.

Now I move into the true mental and physical pre-shot routine for the shot. I stand behind the ball, facing the flag. I'm picturing in my mind the exact trajectory of the shot I'm about to hit, including where it lands and exactly how it either checks up or rolls out. Keeping that picture in my mind, I'll walk up next to the ball and make an 80 percent practice swing, just to get some rhythm and feel in my hands. I'll step back behind the ball, look down at the ball and then out to the target while picturing the path of the shot, and then step in to my stance.

Once I'm in my stance, I'll waggle the club, look down at the ball, look up at my target and let it go. My thought is to swing through the ball and into my finish. The average player tends to swing at the ball and immediately look up to see the result—and a lot of times, it's not good.

From the time I start the process of standing behind the ball and visualizing my shot to the time the ball comes off the club is about fifteen seconds. And you could measure that with a stopwatch and it would be pretty consistent—even as I got later into tournaments.

What the routine does is give your mind a specific and creative job to do during the whole process of hitting the shot. You're making a picture in your head of what you want the ball to do, not what you want your swing to look like. It keeps your mind occupied with something productive instead of letting it fill up with tension and worry about the consequences of a bad shot.

Rory McIlroy was on the wrong side of that at the 2011 Masters. He came into the final round with a four-shot lead over Angel Cabrera, and when it started to get away from him on the 10th hole, he began to rush things. His playing partner, Cabrera, is an extremely fast player, too, and Rory was rushing through his routine and then rushing to his next shot—only to have to wait because the pace was slow.

It all went haywire for him, but there's no shame in any of that. He's incredibly talented, but he was (and still is) a young guy, and there's a process to figuring these things out. He showed how special his talent is two months later at the U.S. Open at Congressional, where he put on a clinic to win his first major. He was in complete control of both his game and his emotions. Just to put an exclamation point on it, I was watching him make the turn there, and he had just made a great 2 on the really tough 10th hole. Play was backed up on the 11th tee, but instead of standing there staring at this intimidating tee shot and letting the tension build, he came back to the 10th green and looked over to the adjacent 18th green so he could get a preview of what was coming later. It was so mature, and the perfect thing to do within his routine. He ended up winning by eight shots.

Good short-game and putting routines cover all of the same bases. For a short-game shot, my routine is devoted to choosing whether I'm going to hit a high shot or a low shot, where exactly I want my ball to land, seeing the full shot in my mind, and then getting into my stance and letting it go.

In putting, my routine is based on walking onto the green to figure out how it drains and what the predominant break is. I then read my putt from behind the ball to determine the break, then go to the low side of the break to see the entire arc of the putt. Then I go back behind the ball. I'll picture the curvature in my mind—including the exact spot on the cup where the putt will enter. From there, I'll move into my stance, set my right foot and then look at my target. Then I'll set the putter in front of the ball and set my left foot. I'll bring the putter over the ball, look down to a spot an inch in front of my ball—on the line I want the putt to travel— and let it go.

The only variances in the routine happen when there's a tricky lie or stance to deal with, either in a full shot or in the short game. In that case, I might take a few more practice swings off to the side in a lie and stance similar to the one for the shot I'm about to hit. I'm trying to test out what the feel of the club through the grass is going to be, so I can be ready for it on the real shot.

I want to stress that you don't have to follow *this* particular routine if it doesn't work for you. The important thing is that you have one, and that it feels comfortable. I worked with Annika Sorenstam, and part of her routine was to make practice swings at the ball. The routine was too long for my taste, and we modified it so that she took the swings parallel to the ball, so that when she was over it she would go right into playing the shot. And some players like to get more feel for a longer putt by stepping up to the line a few feet from the hole and making an imaginary little stroke as if they were putting that short one in, so they can visualize the last few feet of break. Rory modified his routine specifically for Augusta's fast, sloped greens—he first went to the low side, as he normally would, and then he moved around to the high side to picture where the ball would drop into the hole. He was looking for something to give himself a better picture. If it works, I'm for it.

Many, many times, I'll get a call from a tour player who is struggling with his or her putting or short game. I'll make a simple observation about a hiccup in their routine, and they'll immediately click back into rolling it great. I just saw Rory, and he started out by missing three straight putts from about 10 feet. I told him to start over and go through his routine. He did, and he started drilling them right in the heart. We talked about how important it was to practice just enough to keep the routine working and keep his feel and not to start grinding away "working on things." When you disconnect the image of the ball's path into the hole and the feel of the shot from what you're practicing, you're doing more harm than good.

Keep in mind that there's nothing noble about spending

two or three hours on the practice green when all you're doing is ingraining bad habits and routines that don't help you. More isn't automatically better.

Whatever specific routine you establish for yourself, I'd like you to avoid a few common mistakes many players make. Starting with the full swing, a big, big thing to avoid is getting frozen over the ball. A lot of players go through an elaborate routine, and then go completely still and stiff before they begin the swing. They actually tense up to the point that you can see the muscles pop out in their arms. Jack Nicklaus is the perfect example of the opposite—and a guy you want to copy. He never stopped moving in his routine, and he kept his body loose and fluid—which keeps the touch and feel in your hands.

Another common full-swing routine mistake is to set yourself so that the club grounds behind the ball and sticks down in the grass. When you start the backswing, you have to jerk the club back and clear it from the grass, which can start everything off on the wrong note. Again, the thought and feel should be loose, fluid and related to the picture of the shot you're seeing.

On short game shots, the two major issues players have in relation to their routine are locking in on the flag as the target and failing to get a feel for the lie and slope.

As I explained in *Unconscious Scoring*, I separate all of my short-game shots into two categories—high shots and low shots—and I use a basic technique for each one. That massively simplifies the shot selection process, and it lets me visualize one of two distinct trajectories. When you're looking at your shot—high or low—you want to see the entire length of the shot from the time it leaves the club to the specific spot where it lands to where it eventually rolls out. That makes your initial aiming point the landing spot for the shot—not the hole. If your routine is focused on the hole, that's like playing every putt as dead straight. You're giving up a powerful part of the analysis.

It's playing in black and white instead of color.

When you have a short-game shot out of something other than a "standard" good lie from short grass, find a duplicate lie a few steps away from your ball and make a couple of practice swings to see how the clubhead interacts with the grass. It's also a great habit to get into for shots from awkward sidehill, downhill, or uphill lies, because you're giving yourself a preview of how your body needs to respond and stay in balance. The worst thing you can do is to make three or four air practice swings without seeing your shot, then stepping up and hitting the shot without even using a swing that replicates the other one.

The most common issues with a putting routine have to do with practice strokes and setup. The idea of making a practice stroke on the putting green is pretty ingrained in most players. But I've never understood what they actually accomplish. The putter doesn't have to go through any grass, and you're not dealing with any lie or stance issues. And I can accept a practice stroke in somebody's routine—like Annika's—if doing it actually provided a mental benefit to the player. But most players make their read and step up just to the side of the ball. Then they stare down and make a couple of practice strokes in a way that's totally disconnected from the picture of the putt they're about to roll. They're losing the feel for the read they just spent the first part of their routine establishing.

I would like to see a routine that allows a player to make his or her stroke as soon as possible after the read is confirmed and the mind is committed. It seems to me that whenever you add extra time in between, there's just more opportunity for tension and second-guessing to creep in. You can create the same kinds of problems if you get into your setup, stare down at the ball and freeze everything while you think about what you're going to do. It's like connecting yourself to a wall socket that is shooting nothing but pure tension into your muscles. I don't see how that can be good. You wouldn't get up and put the cue stick beside the cue ball you were about to hit in pool and practice it over and over again, would you? You go behind the ball and keep it moving, for feel.

I don't want you to see this concept of building a routine as overwhelming or beyond your capabilities. With a minimal amount of practice, literally anyone can have a framework for a routine that gets the job done. You're not going to get it right every time, and that's OK. Every player is going to be faced with a shot that he or she isn't confident about. You try to protect against your big miss, or you worry about carrying some kind of obstacle or hazard. Your last thought isn't about what you want to happen. It's about what you don't want to happen. It's a problem that creeps in even for tour players. The key is to give yourself that framework to see what's happening and to then make the necessary adjustments.

I was playing an event in Atlanta in 1995—well into my senior career—and I hit a bad tee shot into the deep stuff on the right side of the 18th hole in the second round. We got to the final round, and I was in the final group with Bob Murphy. I came to the 18th tee with a one-shot lead. After what had happened the day before, I knew I didn't want to miss it right. Bob stepped up and hooked one badly to the left, and ended up about a foot inbounds. I was thinking to myself, "Don't miss left, either." So I got up and flat-out topped my tee shot, and hit it about 70 yards. That's what can happen when you start thinking about the shots you don't want to hit instead of seeing what you want the ball to do—even out on tour. I hit a 4-wood down to layup range, wedged it on, saved my par, and won the tournament by a shot.

Remember that just like your swing, your routine doesn't have to be perfect for you to see dramatic improvement overall. Any steps you can take toward adopting a consistent routine are going to pay off for you. And the better you get with your routine, the fewer uncomfortable, nonconfident moments you're going to have.

4
HOW TO LEARN

WHEN I learned to play the game from my dad in the 1950s, golf instruction didn't look or sound anything like what's available to any player—amateur or professional—today. I was extremely lucky to live on a golf course and have unlimited access to my dad, Gail Stockton—who was a pretty well-known golf pro in Southern California.

The lessons my dad taught me consisted of him watching me hit shots and giving me single, simple things to practice, and then sending me off on my own to ingrain those elements into my game before I came back for the next piece. I spent hours and hours knocking the ball around a little circuit of holes near our backyard.

My dad obviously didn't have a TrackMan system, a high-definition video camera, or an iPad to show me the swing I had just made. Magazines like *Golf Digest* and *Golf Magazine* didn't exist yet, and there certainly wasn't a channel on television dedicated 100 percent to the game, like Golf Channel is now.

There's no question that the average person in Anytown, USA, has much, much better access to all different kinds of golf instruction—even compared to just ten years ago. There are flat-out more PGA professionals now, and the average level of knowledge and training in golf instruction is higher than ever before. There's an incredible amount of information available in golf magazines, on television, and on the Internet. You could spend a month straight just watching instruction clips on YouTube.

Overall, I think it's great that there's so much available to the average player.

But to me, it raises a major question.

With all this "stuff" out there, how do you know what will work for you?

I used to tag along with my dad when he went to the range to give lessons to the members at Arrowhead Country Club, in San Bernardino. I'd find a spot at the end of the range to hit balls while he worked. My dad told me over and over again that it was important that I didn't listen to what he was saying to the other players, because what he was prescribing for them wouldn't necessarily work for me. It truly was like watching a doctor work in an emergency room: The process for fixing a broken leg is a lot different than the one to perform open-heart surgery.

And that's really the challenge you face when you're trying to get better. You might get a lesson here and there from a teacher in your town, subscribe to one of the golf magazines, and watch some of the instruction shows on television. You're getting a few things from the teacher, and then adding some of the tips you read or see, and then going out and hoping for the best.

It shouldn't be much of a surprise that this patchwork quilt of ideas doesn't usually hold up under the pressure of playing for real. The more lessons you take, the shorter lifespan those lessons tend to have.

As my career on the PGA Tour continued through the 1960s and 1970s, I became more and more appreciative of what my dad had done for me, both as a young player and a tour pro. What he gave me was a simple, unified way of determining what pieces of information were worth copying and adding into my game, and which were better left alone.

Even more importantly, he showed me that there was a place for mechanical instruction in the game, but that it was far, far more important to feel like I owned my swing—and that my mind was in the right place—so that I would be able analyze my own game and correct my mistakes.

Within a few years of my dad passing away in 1983, my son Ron became my coach. For the year before the Ryder Cup in 1991, I had totally given up playing in any corporate outings, and I basically didn't play much golf. After the matches, I dropped everything and spent five weeks doing nothing but practicing to get ready for my fiftieth birthday, on November 2, when I would be eligible for the Champions Tour.

As a part of that process, Ron and I went to visit Mac O'Grady in Palm Springs—just down the road from our base in Redlands, California. Mac won a couple of times on the PGA Tour in the 1980s, but by the late 1980s had become one of the most respected—if eccentric—experts in the world on the golf swing. Some of us believe the swing is about feel and art, but Mac is a genius about what the body should be doing during a golf swing. I vividly remember playing in a Tuesday practice round in the 1980s in Williamsburg, Virginia, with Mark Pfeil. Mac was supposed to play with us, but he got into a disagreement with his caddie, who left. So Mac ditched his bag and played the entire round with just his 4-iron—using it for everything from tee shots to bunker shots to putts—and shot 2-under. He was a tour-caliber player right-handed, and could turn around left-handed and play at scratch. He certainly had a gift.

Ron and I made the short trip to see Mac with the thought that we could learn something about the golf swing. My dad worked in simple images and pictures, and Mac was the opposite. Mac is heavily influenced by Homer Kelley and *The Golfing Machine,* and he had this sequence of eight positions you needed to get into during the swing— and a blizzard of scientific terminology to describe all of them.

We'd do an hour lesson, and I wouldn't understand a lot of what he was talking about. But Ron and I would get in the car to drive home, and he'd distill what we just did into two minutes of what I needed to know. There's no question my swing got way better with Mac's help—he was talking about the importance of golfers using their core muscles a decade before anybody else—but I needed a teacher with Ron's talent to be able to deliver the information I needed in the form that allowed me to incorporate it.

What Ron was able to do for me—and what you should always be trying to do for your own game—was to determine what was useful and then make it flow into what I was already doing.

It took me about six months to have a feeling of what I was supposed to be doing with my swing. Halfway through the 1992 Champions Tour season, I won the Senior Players Championship outside Detroit, and that started a run where I took the money title in 1993 and 1994, and won thirteen other tournaments and two other majors—including the 1996 U.S. Senior Open.

If you come and see us for a lesson or a clinic, I hope the main takeaway after our time together doesn't center on the way you hold your putter, or how you hit your pitch shots. That might be a bit of the conversation we have, but learning and getting better is way more than just having a teacher watch you and tell you what you're doing wrong. All the advice in this book is designed to help you see things on the course more clearly, and to get more comfortable with your own process and your own swing.

What does that translate into in the real world?

It might be hard to believe at first, but I think most players would do better taking fewer lessons—and a different kind of lesson when they do take one.

Before you get mad at me and say I'm taking food out of

your PGA teacher's mouth or money out of his or her pocket, I want to emphasize that many instructors do a great job. They can be a great help, especially when you're learning the basics of the game.

But the problem is that many players approach golf instruction with the idea that they need to "perfect" what they're doing. They become professional lesson-takers—constantly searching for the tip or piece of swing advice that is going turn them into a ballstriking machine.

When you consider how the brain actually works, it's easy to see why those players never see any real improvement. It takes about two to three weeks of practice and focus on one specific motion to move it from the conscious mind—where you have to specifically focus on doing it—to the subconscious. In other words, if you adjust your grip, it takes a few weeks of consciously making the new grip with your hands, checking it to make sure it's correct, and then hitting shots with it before the new grip starts to become a regular part of what you "automatically" do.

And until you can go out and hit shots on the golf course without having the different physical pieces of your swing occupy the center of your mind, you're not going to play your best golf. That's just as true for a guy trying to win the Masters as it is for somebody trying to break 100 for the first time. Whatever kind of swing you have, it's going to work better if your concentration is on where you want the ball to go—not on what to do with your hands, how much to turn or any other conscious physical controlling of your body. Remember, Byron Nelson played the entire 1945 season—when he won eleven tournaments in a row and eighteen overall—with just a single swing thought.

Think about your game in that context. Now imagine what happens when you go out and take a bunch of lessons back to back. It's natural to equate the total number of hours you spend on lessons and hitting balls to getting better, but that's just not the case. Unless you give yourself time to let each individual lesson "take," you're just confusing yourself. You're trapping your game in the conscious mode.

I used to get so frustrated with my dad when he would give me a simple thing to work on with my swing and then send me away for a few weeks to work on it. Of course, I'd go out and hit a bucket of balls and be convinced that I had it and was ready for the next piece, only to have him ignore me when I asked for more information. He knew that each piece of the puzzle needed time.

As I said before, there are lots of great teachers out there. And the technology that's available can show you lots of new information about your swing. But to find the right teacher for *you,* the same principles hold true today as they did when I was getting those lessons from my dad in the 1950s.

First, does your teacher make you feel comfortable? Does he or she understand what you're trying to accomplish, and do they make you feel good about coming and getting help? After all, you're spending good money to get the lesson—and you're getting the lesson to perform better and get more enjoyment out of what for most people is something they do for fun and recreation during their free time. It would be silly to pay money to spend time with a teacher who made you feel miserable—and didn't actually help you shoot better scores.

When I'm working with a student, my focus is on trying to get them to engage with their sense of feel. How does the club feel in their hands? What does something simple like a waggle do to enhance the feel of the clubhead before a swing? I'm trying to match what the person does in their short game and putting with their personal signature. I'm trying to free them up to do what they can naturally do. The best words I can hear a player say to me are, "This feels different," because feel equals feedback. If you can feel the difference between the different things you're doing, you're learning. The next thing they usually say after that is, "This feels like it used to." Amateur players usually get done with a lesson and say, "I can't believe it's that simple."

We'll go through this process with tour players and some of them will immediately want to book another day of lessons, because they believe that "more" will translate into "better." But the reality is that virtually every lesson I give is about forty minutes—max. Then we'll move on to the bunker or short game and do another forty minutes.

Putting and short-game problems are usually less complicated than full-swing ones, but the bigger point is that if something takes longer than thirty or forty minutes to get across, it's something that's too complicated to be bundled together in one lesson.

It's extremely important to talk to your teacher about the overall plan for what you're trying to accomplish, and to see the steps in front of you. That way, both of you can control the pace of the information. You can ask which pieces are the most important in the progression, and you can devote your practice time to the first one before moving on to No. 2 or No. 3. And, as my dad tried to get me to understand all those years ago, the steps and advice are going to be different for you than they will be for the next guy.

Watch any PGA or LPGA Tour event and you'll immediately see than not every guy and girl is built the same or swings the same. A good teacher won't try to fit you into a style or "system" that isn't compatible with your body type, flexibility, ability, or level of athleticism. There's no shame in being up front about the fact that you aren't as strong or as flexible as Dustin Johnson. Maybe three people in the world are. It doesn't make much sense to try to swing a driver like he does—even though you wish you could!

On a more basic level, maybe your personality and body type are closer to a fast, slashing type of player like Seve Ballesteros. Or maybe you reroute the club like Jim Furyk does. That's perfectly acceptable. If you're going to pattern your game after somebody, pick somebody you feel comfortable copying. This isn't just advice for an amateur player. I'd tell a player like Michelle Wie the same thing. When you watch her, it's obvious she's trying to play like Tiger Woods. She practices for hours and hours, bless her heart, trying to grind greatness out. But what she really needs to do is to go back in time. She has all the talent in the world—and all this creativity and flair. She needs to go out and play like Rory McIlroy. She should go out there and just let it go. She needs to play like an artist, not an engineer.

It isn't a surprise to me that so many amateurs struggle with this grind-it-out, focus-on-mechanics mentality. Amateurs watch the pros. And in many cases, what the pros do with their games and routines isn't good at all. You'll see them on the range, making a backswing and looking back to see the exact location of the club. Or they'll be out playing and get to a big shot and all of a sudden make an additional five or six slow practice swings. It reinforces the swing obsession instead of what I think is the most important factor: the visual of the shot. When you watch guys who understand this and play free—guys like Brandt Snedeker or Lee Trevino—it's such a joy. They get up there and let it go.

And that's really what it comes down to. At the end of the day, you can hit balls forever on the practice range, but all that work doesn't mean anything if you can't take it to the course. At some point, you have to transition from hitting practice balls—where there are no consequences—to hitting real shots on real holes.

Now, I know it isn't as easy as reading this paragraph and flipping a switch, but you can make the transition smoother if you change some of your practice sessions from mindlessly pounding balls to going out and playing a nine-hole practice round. The practice round aspect removes the score pressure, but actually being out on the golf course and hitting one ball instead of twenty gives you the look and feel of a real shot. The routine out on tour when I played used to be full eighteen-hole practice rounds with guys you liked, complete with some money matches to keep things interesting. Now, more and more players are getting to tournaments where they know the course and playing nine-hole practice rounds by themselves, hitting to locations where they know the pins are going to be. They're re-creating what they're going to see under tournament conditions. It's the best kind of practice there is. At the tour level, physically hitting the shots isn't nearly as important as getting mentally prepared for the tournament. In 2008, Yani Tseng was an LPGA rookie who had never won a tournament. She showed up at the LPGA Championship on Monday with a terrible case of the flu. Her people wanted her to come out and play a practice round so she could learn the course, but Ron sent her right back to the hotel. She rested, and in the afternoon they walked the course together while she carried just a putter. They plotted strategy and hit a few putts to get a feel for the greens, but that was the extent of her practice round. He knew she needed to be both mentally prepared to play and in the best physical condition she could be. She went on to win her first tournament—and first major championship—that week.

Even if you don't have time to play nine practice holes at your course, set up your practice so you're being creative and seeing shots, not just mindlessly hitting balls out of a pile. Phil Mickelson uses just four balls in his short-game practice routine. He finds a certain shot and certain lie, hits four shots and watches each one intently, then picks up the balls himself and moves to a different spot. He'll go from low shots to high shots out of deeper grass to bunker shots, hitting four balls at a time. It's a great, great way to work on seeing and feeling different shots. You're adding "golf course feel" to your routine and making it feel more natural.

Once you've built a good rapport with your teacher, lessons don't even have to happen at the golf course. My dad was great about asking me really specific questions about what was happening with my game. By the time I got to the tour, he was able to listen to my descriptions and give me great guidance—without seeing me hit a single shot. I might say to him that every shot felt thin to me, and I was missing to the right. He'd say that it sounded like I was swaying off the ball. My center was moving back, and it was causing me to hang back and swing up on the ball. If I stayed centered, my height in relation to the ball would return and I'd start compressing the ball again. I'd go and hit some balls with that single, simple swing thought—stay centered—and my ballstriking would come back.

It works the same way with players like Mickelson today. I might have spent a total of forty-five minutes with Phil last year. We've gone through everything already, and we use our visits so that he can get another set of eyes to confirm what he sees. For example, he texted me to say he wasn't getting the feel of the clubhead coming through the sand the way he liked. I watched him hit two shots, and I saw his knees were moving back on the backswing. I told him to keep his weight forward and post on his lead leg. He hit two more shots and said, "Ahh!" It clicked right back in.

A lot of the players we've worked with have come for a few lessons, gotten what they needed, and moved on. I don't take it as an insult, or feel like I've been used. We're trying to teach players to be their own teachers—which, by definition, would make them less reliant on lessons. If a guy like Justin

Rose can come see us—like he did with Dave Jr. in 2012—and use what we share to play better, that's what we're trying to accomplish. Justin won two of the next three events he played after seeing Junior. We haven't seen him since then, but he used elements of what he learned in his green reading and routine when he won the U.S. Open at Merion in 2013. He picked our brains and put it to good use. That's success, for everybody. Tom Kite used to amaze me at the way he could take lessons from a bunch of different people and take something useful from everybody he saw. He worked with Harvey Penick, Chuck Cook, and Bob Rotella, and with me on his short game. He was able to work with a vast assortment of people, but he never got confused.

One question I get asked a lot is if it's hard to integrate some of the things I teach about putting and the short game with the things taught by a player's full-swing instructor. To me, it's not an issue. There's more specialization in instruction now than ever before. A tour player can have a mental game coach, a putting coach, a swing coach, a trainer, and a dietitian. All of those people have to work for the team. The economics of the tour certainly support that at the highest level—the guy who finished fifth at the Players Championship won more money than Ben Hogan did in his whole career—and that concept of specialization is starting to trickle into the amateur game as well.

You're fortunate if you have a teacher who has real expertise in both the full swing and the other pieces of the game. During my years at TaylorMade, I enjoyed watching Jim Flick working at the back of the range at the test center with a procession of amateurs and pros. There are so many components to it—from short game to full swing to strategy to clubfitting. It's hard to be great at everything. There's no question that teachers like Butch Harmon, David Leadbetter, and Sean Foley are terrific at fixing golf swings. They're experts there, and we're experts around and on the green. A good teacher might not love it if you're also seeing another teacher, but he or she will understand if you're going to another person for putting help or bunker help or short-game advice. After all, the end goal is improvement.

If you do have a teacher with a balanced set of skills— meaning that he or she also has some experience competing— keep in mind that there are ways for him or her to help you that don't involve the practice range. Go and invite your pro to lunch one day, and pay for both the lunch and an hour of instruction. Spend that time just talking about course strategies. Not only does he or she know your game better than anybody, they also know how to attack a golf course. You'll walk away from the lunch with a blueprint of how to play each hole at your home course. It's an element of the game that is almost completely overlooked. Some of the best clinics we've ever had came when we were rained out and we all sat inside talking about strategy and other mental-game components. People weren't getting distracted by watching the ball.

Another reason to get a lesson is to track your improvement within the context of your equipment. If you're getting better, you're probably going to need to get refit for your putter, irons and driver. After a putting lesson, raising or lowering your hands or incorporating more of a forward press means that the club needs to be bent or changed. More club-head speed equals a different shaft flex in your irons and a new kick point in your driver shaft.

Those aren't bad problems to have.

5

HOW TO EVALUATE
YOURSELF

WHEN I first went out onto the PGA Tour, back in the dark ages, we obviously didn't have smartphones with built-in video cameras, notebooks, and calendars. And the tour barely kept track of even basic stats like driving distance and putting average. Unless you and your caddie did some work on your own, the only thing you knew for sure about your game was what your scoring average was and how much money you made.

I knew I had some work to do. I needed more information so I could determine very specifically what parts of my game I needed to improve.

I tell this story because the average amateur player today actually has *more* access to accurate information about his or her game than I had in 1965. You don't need to have access to the PGA Tour's sophisticated ShotLink measurement system to develop a comprehensive database of information about the shots you hit. And once you have that information, you can use it for everything from improving your decision-making to getting a lesson to improve your technique in a certain aspect of your game.

Let's start by talking about just what kind of information is good to know.

From my first year on tour, I compiled my own annual book of statistics about my play during tournaments, and kept it in a little stenographer pad I tucked in my golf bag. I counted fairways and greens hit, whether my misses off the tee were right or left, and whether I was long or short on approach shots. On and around the green, I kept track of my number of putts—which was a deceptive number, because I tended to miss more greens than the average tour player. I had a lot of one-putt greens because my short game and putting tended to be very good. I also kept track of my up-and-down percentage from the sand.

Information like that made it possible for me to see trends in my game. If I had a run of rounds where I was missing a lot of tee shots to the right, I could do something about it—even if that just meant adjusting my aim. At the end of the season, I compiled all of the information into one report, which gave me my basic statistical breakdown for the season.

During my time off in the winter, I'd be sitting in a duck blind in the peace and quiet, and all of a sudden I'd get some great ideas about what to do with my game for the next season. I was able to do this because I took a break from the game and focused my mind on something else. That balance is so important. To look back and reflect, you actually have to give yourself the time and room to do it. When you're concentrating on one thing week to week, information can kind of blur together. You can have the opposite problem, too. If you don't play much, keeping stats and notes will help you get back to where you were the last time.

But the actual record-keeping aspect of stats, like greens in regulation and fairways hit, is just one part of the overall strategy you need to evaluate your game. Those measurements have to work in tandem with a tangible set of long-term goals. On tour, the time frame is pretty straightforward—a set of goals for a full season. For you, your time frame might be three months, six months, or a year. The goal component is a crucial part of the evaluation process, because the act of establishing goals—and the quality of the goals you set—is a huge indicator of what you measure and how you interpret the information.

I'll give you an example.

In an average season on the Champions Tour in the 1990s, I made a series of goals that looked something like this:

1. Enjoy yourself

2. Lead the birdie statistics

3. Improve miss tendencies

Notice that I didn't have any scoring-average goals, money goals or victory goals. I made my list short, and totally focused on positive outcomes. The first goal, enjoying myself, didn't have anything to do with statistics, but it was the most important one to me. If I was going to be on the road and away from my family for sixteen to eighteen weeks, I darn sure better be having a good time out there. That meant playing practice rounds with guys I liked, having dinner with interesting people, and refusing to let bad rounds carry over to the next day in my attitude.

The second goal, leading the birdie statistics, is influenced by many other factors. Overall, wanting to lead the tour in birdies is a statement about how aggressively you decide to play. If you want to make a lot of birdies, you're going to have to go at some pins that will produce a bogey (or worse) if you miss. That meant I needed to be more accurate off the tee so that I had reasonable shots from the fairway; my proximity-to-the-hole number needed to be good; and my putting needed to be right there. All of those factors (and a bunch more) go into making more raw birdies—it's not just about shooting lower scores.

The third goal, improving my miss tendencies, had to do with being aware of my game from week to week and staying on top of it. If I was missing a lot of fairways to the right, I would be foolish not to notice that trend and at least change my aiming point off the tee. If my shots weren't consistently getting pin high, I would know I needed to adjust my club selection.

Actually meeting the goals isn't as important as setting them. Once you've set the target, you record your progress by measuring and evaluating your game.

What goals should you pick? That's obviously a personal choice, but I believe you need a combination of tangible and intangible goals, as well as a combination of relatively easy-to-achieve ones and some that are a stretch. You don't want to set an easy, low bar that doesn't push you, and the opposite is true as well. If all of your goals are completely out of reach, you're going to get discouraged and stop trying.

I can still remember asking my son Dave Jr. about his goals as he was trying to get out onto the PGA Tour one year. He said his goal was to prepare to go to qualifying school by working on specific parts of his game, then get to the Q-School finals and win that tournament. And that's exactly what he did. Not only did he win two tournaments on the Web.com Tour (which was called the Nike Tour then), he also tied for first in the Q-School finals and earned his tour card for the 1994 season.

To evaluate your own game, break it down into those two parts. Pick a combination of goals, and then get an accurate set of information about how you actually play. You definitely don't need the tour's ShotLink system to keep track of what you actually do. You can use any number of free or really low-cost apps they sell for your smartphone, or even just a pencil and your scorecard.

Start with the basics—fairways and greens hit. Along with your handicap, those percentages are a good overall barometer of how you're hitting full shots with the driver and irons. As I was saying above, it's good to know the number of putts you take during a round—and I define that as the actual number of shots you take using your putter, even if you're just off the green—but you need to keep that number in context with all the other aspects of your game. I can't tell you the number of amateur players I've worked with who show up the first day and tell me what an awful putter they are. They're ready with a story about how many times they've been three-putting lately. That's fine, and there might be some work to do on putting, but a good chunk of those three-putts could be caused by hitting a lot of iron shots onto the green that end up far away from the hole, or having a short game that isn't up to snuff. If you're hitting bad chips and leaving yourself a lot of 40-footers, you're going to three-putt some, even if you're on the PGA Tour.

You're going to gain a tremendous amount of information about your game if you keep more detailed short-game records, too. A good baseline stat to know is your overall up-and-down percentage from 30 yards and in. That's a total percentage for every short-game shot you hit inside 30 yards, whether it's from the fairway, rough, or sand. If that number starts to drop, it gives you reason to investigate a number of things. Is your decision-making poor, so that you're leaving yourself a lot of really hard short-game shots? Do you need some work on a particular kind of short-game shot? Knowing your percentage strictly from the sand works in tandem with the overall stat, and if a lot of those misses are coming from the bunker, you know where you need to devote your time.

Once you have some experience keeping track of your basic tendencies, you can branch out into the next level of information. Where are your misses off the tee? Left? Right? What clubs are you using on approach shots, and what is your miss tendency for each of them? If you're hitting great shots with your 6-, 8- and 9-irons but your 7-iron is off, that can tell you something about the way the 7-iron is built compared to the other ones. If your misses are relatively consistent—say, short and right—at minimum you have another piece of information to plug into your decision-making process when you're pulling a club. If your miss is a short right shot and there's a huge bunker short and right of the green, you might need to pick a different club and a different aiming point.

I know that some of the data experts out there have come up with composite statistics showing how many fairways and greens the "average" player at different handicap levels hits. It's interesting to know that an "average" 18-handicap hits 3.5 greens per round, but that doesn't apply to your game. The critical part for you is to go out and measure where you are and then keep track of where you're trending. Where you stand isn't as important as where you're headed. If you're hitting one green per round, you need to keep in mind that a day when you hit two is a good day—not that you *only* hit two greens.

The whole goal of this exercise is to become more aware of what is happening when you play. And I don't mean what's happening with the physical movement of your club. I'm talking about the pattern of shots you're actually hitting. I firmly believe that the only bad golfers are golfers who don't see the mistakes they make and try to fix them. That's as true for a 36-handicapper who isn't consistently getting the ball off the ground as it is for a PGA Tour player. The only way to get better is to understand what needs improving. It certainly comes easier for some people. My son Dave was caddying for me at Quad Cities in the early 1980s, when he was thirteen or fourteen years old. I made a really nice 2 on the fifth hole in the pro-am on Wednesday, and he asked me about it when we got into the car. He told me I hit the wrong shot into the green—that it should have been a low one to get back to the back pin. The number on my scorecard was good, but a closer look at the shot I hit showed me where I had room to make a better decision.

I've played hundreds of pro-am rounds where my amateur partner rolled a bad first putt that went well past the hole, but was then so mad or embarrassed about the putt that he looked away in disgust and missed seeing what the ball did as it went by the hole. Watching the ball go by gives you more information about what it will do on the return putt coming up. Or I'll watch a guy just burning up over a three-putt, and he's so mad at himself that he isn't thinking about what led up to it—say, picking the wrong club from 120 yards in the middle of the fairway.

That's a lost opportunity.

Three weeks before I won my first PGA Tour event at Colonial, I was playing at the Greensboro Open and missed a tee shot badly to the left on the first hole of the final round to basically give away my lead. At Colonial on Sunday, I was feeling pretty nervous as the leader. My dad was walking with me as I headed toward the first tee and suggested I aim down the right center and try to hit a fade. I got up there and thought about what my dad said, then aimed down the right center of the fairway with the thought that I was going to hit a nice little fade. And darn it if the shot didn't come off as a perfect little draw that ended up in the left center of the fairway. It was the right combination of swing thought and accounting for my potential for a miss under pressure. If I had just gotten up there and done my normal thing, I probably would have snap hooked it and made a big score. My day would have started a lot differently—and negatively—than with the routine par I ended up making.

6

HOW TO BELIEVE
IN YOURSELF

YOU could dedicate an entire spare bedroom in your house to shelves of books dedicated to the concept of positive thinking and the power the mind has to influence your physical results. Everybody from Norman Vincent Peale (*The Power of Positive Thinking*) to Maxwell Maltz (*Psycho-Cybernetics*) to Dr. Bob Rotella (*Golf Is a Game of Confidence*) has something to say on the subject.

The "rah-rah" cheerleader aspect of a lot of that advice can turn some people off—and some people hear it and automatically dismiss it because they don't think it applies to them. "It's easy to tell somebody to believe in themselves if they're a great player . . ." or "What good is positive thinking going to do me when I'm just going to hit a bad shot anyway?" are two common responses I hear at clinics and outings.

I'm not here to give you a halftime speech about changing your attitude. I want to tell you about the real situations that all different kinds of players—from those on the PGA Tour to those at your club down the street—find themselves in, and the mental triggers that get you in trouble out on the course but can also help restore your mental and emotional balance.

It isn't magic. It's simple psychology. And it works for major championship winners and 30-handicappers in the same way.

In the summer of 2012, Rory McIlroy was going through a slump. He missed the cut at the U.S. Open as the defending champion, then tied for 60th at the British Open. Before the World Golf Championship event at Firestone the week before the PGA, he and I had a quick chat on the practice green. It didn't have anything to do with mechanics or green reading or strategy. I told him that I wanted him to go out that week and play with a smile on his face. I wanted to be able to watch him on television and not be able to tell whether he had made a birdie on the last hole or a double bogey. I reminded him that playing golf was all he ever wanted to do, and that there was no advantage to getting upset on the course. I wanted him to enjoy himself.

He went out and shot 67-68 on the weekend at Akron to finish tied for fifth, then lapped everybody at Kiawah Island the next week at the PGA Championship to win his second major—by eight shots, the same margin as his U.S. Open victory the year before. In his press conference on Sunday night, he was gracious enough to point to our conversation as the trigger point that reminded him to get back to enjoying the game.

I'm not trying to tell you that chanting some positive script to yourself over and over again on the first tee is going to instantly transform you into Rory McIlroy. The main thing to take away from this story is how easy it is for even the best players in the world to lose confidence and stop enjoying the game—and how simple it can be to get it back. Your "mental health" is something you need to constantly monitor in your game—regardless of your handicap level— just like you keep running tabs on how you're hitting your driver or rolling your putts.

The fact that players like Rory and Tiger Woods and Yani Tseng can go through crises of confidence proves that nobody is immune. But the beauty of the mental game is that it doesn't take freak athletic ability or six thousand range balls to improve it. Anybody can use a variety of strategies to play with more confidence. My goal here is to show you how to identify when you're going to a bad place mentally, and how to pull yourself out of that cycle when it happens. You don't have to be perfect to get something out of it, either— and you don't have to grind away for hours. Small improvements will show up right away on your scorecard.

The first element of confidence is related to the story I just told about Rory McIlroy. It has to do with the running conversation you have with yourself when you're out playing. Psychologists call this inner monologue "self-talk," and it has a dramatic impact on both your physical and mental performance—and not just on the golf course.

One of the main reasons that Maxwell Maltz began to research the ideas behind his *Psycho-Cybernetics* book was that some of his plastic surgery patients were having persistent problems after they left the hospital—problems unrelated to any physical complications from the surgery. A certain percentage of patients weren't satisfied with the surgery even though it would be measured a success by every reasonable standard. They had come to a surgeon to correct a problem, but even after it was corrected, they weren't happy. Maltz's theory was that the patients sabotaged their potential for being happy about the results of the surgery with an avalanche of negative self-talk.

What does a bunch of unhappy surgery patients have to do with golf? Everything.

Most people who play this game get it backward. They hit some bad shots—either on the range or out on the course—and they get angry at themselves. They set up the next shot pretty much expecting to hit another bad one, and when they do, they just let themselves have it—with both mental and verbal self-talk.

How many times have you played with somebody who pulled the cart up to the tee and made a comment about how hard a certain tee shot was because of all the trouble down the right side (or left, or wherever it might be)? Then, after a few nervous practice swings, he or she hits the ball into that trouble and says, "I *knew* I was going to do that! I'm terrible!" (Or maybe some even more colorful language. . . .)

It doesn't take that kind of mind-set long to produce exactly what every player is trying to avoid. In other words, the negative self-talk isn't a *result* of hitting bad shots. The negative self-talk is *producing* the bad shots!

Rory McIlroy didn't suddenly forget how to hit golf shots. And you haven't, either. When you get a bad result, it can happen for a bunch of different reasons. But I can tell you that no player—not me, not you, not Rory McIlroy—can play effective golf with a constant stream of negative or angry thoughts.

I call it thinking backward, because your real mental-game goal should be to approach every shot with positive self-talk—with the firm idea that thinking and seeing the shot you want to hit will put you in position to actually do it. The good thinking comes first and produces the result.

Now, I don't live in a fantasyland where anybody can flick a switch and turn off fear or anger just by reading a few words in this book. It takes practice—and you're not always going to get it right.

But the beauty of approaching your game from this "opposite" direction is that you don't have to be perfect at it to see those results. As I said above, *any* improvement is going to show up in your score. If you can start by getting yourself out of the negative self-talk trap for one more shot per round, then one more shot per nine, you'll be a stronger player mentally.

As a first step, tell yourself you're not going to call yourself any more names on the golf course. You can still get angry, and certain shots can still make you nervous, but make a pact that you're done telling yourself (or your cart mate) that you suck, or that you're the worst putter of all time, or that you'll never be able to hit a good tee shot for the rest of your life. The better job you can do of clearing that stuff out of your head, the easier it'll be for you to use the second part of the strategy—visualization—which we're going to talk about in a minute.

Once you've choked off most of the direct insults, start to put some parameters on your emotional reactions to your shots—good and bad. My son Ron uses a great rule of thumb when he teaches on tour. He tells the players to feel free to express anger—or joy—at a shot, but to get it all out of the system from the time the ball leaves the club to when they're twenty steps away from the area of the next shot. Jack Nicklaus could be a role model for a lot of different parts of the game, but he was particularly strong this way. In all the times I played with him or watched him, I never saw him get overcome by emotion—positive or negative. It always looked like things were going just as he thought they would.

Negative self-talk is so devastating because it sucks your confidence away and makes it easy to string a series of bad shots together. When you hit a spectacularly terrible tee shot, the easy response is to get mad or disgusted—or to basically give up on the hole. And that's when you go into the trees and try to muscle one out through a tiny hole in the branches, or you top another one and don't get out of jail. The shot right after a bad one is when you need your most positive outlook and focus, and most people give it the least. They pile up mental mistakes on top of one another, then look down at the card on the next tee and see a triple in the box.

I'm not going to sugarcoat anything. Golf is an incredibly hard game. I played more than nine hundred tournaments on the PGA and Champions tours, and I won twenty-four times. You're going to have a lot more losses than wins. They have a fully exempt PGA Tour now, where 150 guys know they're going to get at least twenty-five or thirty starts per year. But when I was coming out, if you weren't in the top 60 on the money list from the previous year or a winner during the current season, you had to play in the weekly qualifying tournament on Monday—ninety guys for forty or fifty spots. My second year out on tour, I would go four or five weeks in a row and miss out on a spot. All you could do was get in the car and drive to the next tournament site and try to find some place to practice. The lowest time for me was in Houston that year. I shot 62 in a practice round on Sunday to break the course record, but the next day I bogeyed the last five holes to shoot 77 and miss qualifying by a shot.

The only things I could control were in my own mind—trying my best and not giving up. I was a fighter. If the best I could do was 75, so be it. But if I had a chance to go low, I was ready to do that. I enjoyed that mental challenge. I couldn't control what other players were going to shoot, and if I made a bad score on a hole or for a round, there was no way to go back and change it. The only thing I could do was to look forward to the next round and my next chance.

Within the context of your own game, try to get to a place where you're looking forward to hitting the next shot. Be excited by the chance to hit the next one great. And the best part about golf is that you'll always get another chance.

Most of us aren't out there playing with millions of dollars on the line and millions of people watching. So you can't let your self-worth get tied up in what you did on your last hole or your last round. I play with people in pro-ams and they've paid $5,000 just to be there. They have another $5,000 invested in their clubs and clothes. Instead of looking around at the incredible scenery and enjoying an experience most people never get to have, they play terribly because they're so nervous and unhappy. And yet, if you asked them, they'd tell you that they love the game.

I'm not suggesting that you quit being concerned about your score, or that improving isn't important. I want you to leave the course each time with some ideas about where your game is headed. Just don't lose sight of the fact that we're supposed to be doing this because we love it, and because it's a fantastic way to spend free time. You can see beautiful places and meet incredible people.

We talked a lot in Chapter 3 about the value of a routine when it comes to playing under pressure. The second major element of self-belief—visualization—ties into that same story line. Negative thoughts, negative self-talk, and a loss of confidence can happen when you don't occupy your mind with the right things between shots. You start to see the things you don't want to happen instead of the shots you want to hit.

The art of visualization is picturing in your head exactly what you want to happen and then letting your body go on a kind of autopilot and produce what you see.

If you don't have any experience with visualization, I re-alize that it probably sounds kind of far-fetched. But I can tell you from decades of experience playing with and teaching 20-handicappers that it is remarkable how much any player can improve his or her results just by picking a single shot, seeing it happen in their mind's eye, and then replicating it.

How?

Take a small bucket of balls to the range. Instead of rifling thirty of them out there as fast as you can hit them, pick one ball. Now go through your normal pre-shot routine. Hit the shot and hold your finish until the ball hits the ground. Watch how it flies through the air. How high did it go? Did it curve? Where did it land compared to where you thought it would? Most people don't get that far, because they fall back after the finish and then immediately look down to pull the next ball from the pile.

Go through your routine and examine what happens as you hit each ball in the bucket. Actually seeing what your "stock" driver or 7-iron shot looks like is the first step to being able to overlay the vision of that shot onto the hole you're playing.

I remember watching the Mahre brothers—Phil and Steve—ski at the 1984 Winter Olympics in Sarajevo. At the top of the mountain, as they got ready in the gate, they would close their eyes and go through the entire course in their mind. They were visualizing how they were going to go down the hill—looking gates ahead, at the big picture.

That resonated with me, because I had my best results on both the regular and Champions tours when I was able to get into that fully immersed visualizing mind-set. At the 1970 PGA Championship, I wasn't exactly a household name. I had won four times at that point, but I wasn't among the favorites that week at Southern Hills. But when I played my first practice round on Monday, I visualized a huge gallery of people following me all the way around. When I got to the last hole, which was in a natural amphitheater, I pictured those hills as being filled with cheering fans waving me home, and I pictured myself as having already won the tournament.

It turned out almost exactly as I had pictured it. There were plenty of screaming fans—and most of them were screaming for Arnold Palmer. One guy yelled at me to shank it on the 7th hole. I promptly holed a pitching wedge from more than 100 yards for eagle. Another guy cheered when I hit a shot into the lake on the 13th. I dropped and had a really hard pitch shot to a pin on the top of a ridge. I hit it to a foot to save a good bogey. On 18, I stepped onto the tee with a three-shot lead over Arnold and Bob Murphy. I hit a perfect tee shot right down the middle, laid up to take the front bunker out of play, and made a routine bogey to win by two.

You don't have to picture yourself playing Amen Corner at Augusta against Tiger Woods to get the benefit of what I'm talking about. Try this little exercise. Take a sleeve of balls and go out and play a few practice holes. On each shot, try to preview in your mind what the ball is going to do. Remember, you don't have to come up with some 320-yard hero tee shot in your head and get discouraged. Just see the actual shot you want to hit with your own swing and your own game.

It's not a straight shot? So what? Picture your 10-yard cut. How high is it going to go? Where is it going to land out there? How far is it going to roll out? If you're on a par-3, or facing an approach shot, take three clubs over to your ball and picture how each one would fly and where it would end up. Pick the one that matches the shot that works the best. Now go through your routine with just that picture of the shot in your head, make your swing, and copy that shot. You won't always accomplish it, but you'll start doing it more and more.

And you'll start playing in color, instead of black and white.

7

THE ESSENTIALS
OF STRATEGY

SO far, we've spent a lot of time talking about important ways to build the mental side of your game on each shot you hit. Now we're going to discuss how to link those shots together out on the golf course.

The strategy you use to tackle each hole and the decisions you make before every shot are two of the most critical elements to actually *playing* the game. If you have a sound strategy that plays to your strengths and ability level and you make the right decisions for each situation, you're going to get the absolute most out of your game. Golf is about the number on the scorecard—and enjoying the process—not about how a video of your swing or putting stroke compares to some ideal from the professional tours.

I'll prove it to you.

Take the advice from this chapter and go out and play this afternoon. I'll bet you score better immediately, just by paying attention to some of the subtle—and not so subtle—strategy and decision-making advice I'm about to give you.

I know you will, because I see it almost every single week.

In the last pro-am I played in, we started on a 180-yard par-3 with a big pond in front of the green. I usually keep quiet for the first hole or two to get a feel for my group and each player's particular game, so I watched my cart partner go through his whole process for the tee shot.

He determined the distance from the yardage book on the cart, and went back and pulled his 180-yard club from the bag—in this case, an intermediate hybrid. He took four practice swings off to the side of his ball and then lined up so he was aimed directly at the flag. He proceeded to dump a weak fade into the front of the pond.

The problem with that result—aside from the triple-bogey on the scorecard—was that he came down on himself for making a bad swing.

But the reality is that he made a series of bad decisions that pretty much predetermined a negative result. To start, he didn't see his personal shot shape fitting a real shot on that hole before he actually swung the club. He didn't see that shape, pick the right club for that distance and shot shape, and then pick the part of the tee box from which he had the best chance for success.

In this case, he pulled one club, walked to the side of the tee box closest to the cart, aimed at the flag and made a bunch of practice swings to give himself time to get more and more nervous. Sure, he might have made a miraculous swing once out of twenty tries and hit the ball on the green. But everybody in the group knew where the shot was probably going to go.

And that's where it went.

To maximize your chances for a good score on a given hole, you have to start seeing each hole as a combination of shots you know you can play.

Think about the first hole at the course you usually play.

Looking down the fairway from the tee, is there trouble on one side or the other? Out-of-bounds? Water? Deep rough? Is it a straight hole, or does it curve to the left or to the right? Is the green complex built in a way that gives you an easier approach from one side or the other?

The answers to all of those questions are going to help you determine what to do off the tee.

I'm not trying to make it sound like you need to be able to work the ball in either direction at will. In fact, it's the opposite. If most of your tee shots slice 10 yards and go 220 yards in total distance, you can use that knowledge to pick an aiming point off the tee and a strategy for almost any hole.

Let's say you're the player who hits that 220-yard tee shot we just talked about. If you're playing a 370-yard par-4 that doglegs slightly to the right and has a pond to the front left of the green, you're going to want to be as close to the right edge of the fairway as possible off the tee. In that case, you would want to picture a shot that starts down the left edge of the fairway and cuts back across the center, ending up near the inside corner of the dogleg. Depending on how wide the tee box is, you're probably going to have a much better look at that shot if you play it from the far right side of the tee box. It's all about optics and geometry—setting up to a shot that looks good in your mind's eye and picking a line that gives your preferred ball flight the best chance for a safe trip.

I choose my position in the tee box based on the shot shape I like to hit—a draw—and where the flag is on the green. Depending on the amount of curve I see on the shot and how aggressive I plan to be with my swing, I'll either set up on the left side of the tee box, aim at the right edge of the fairway and draw it to the fat part of the fairway, or I'll set up on the right side of the tee box, hit what feels like a straight shot and let it curl into the right edge of the fairway. It all depends on where the flag is on the green and where the trouble is located off the tee. I want to set myself up for the easiest path to the hole.

Once you get to your ball, the process is similar, but with a few more factors added in. Can you carry the ball to the green, or do you need to run it on? If you need to run it on, where do you need to start the ball so that it curves away from the pond on the front left and has a chance to roll up?

If you can carry it to the green, where is the flag? Is it close to the water on the front left? If you curve the ball left to right, that's going to mean you pretty much ignore the flag and try to hit it in the middle of the green. How far up or back is the flag from the center? Is it uphill or downhill from where you are? What is the wind doing? Where is the best place for a bad shot to finish? If I had a dollar for every time one of my partners in a pro-am took one look at the 150-yard marker, pulled one club and went up and hacked at it without another thought, I'm sure I could buy a small island!

Using our original example, if you hit your stock 220-yard tee shot, you'd be 150 yards to the middle of the green. If the green is 30 to 35 yards from front to back, that's a difference of three clubs. Assuming you get the actual distance to your target—call it 143 yards—you should walk up to your ball thinking about the two clubs you could hit for the shot. Go through the scenarios we just discussed—where the flag is, the trouble spots around the green, what the wind is doing. And remember, modern architects know that most players don't take enough club to reach the green. That's why a majority of the trouble you see is parallel to the middle of the green or in front of it. That should influence you to err on the side of more club versus less.

Before you pick your club, you should survey the entire green area to get a sense for where the good and bad places to end up are. For example, when the flag is front right and there's deep rough short and right of the green, you're going to want to pick a club that will carry at least to the flag if you make average contact. The worst that could happen is that you absolutely flush it and it rolls to the back of the green. You're still in better shape than you would be if you were facing a shot out of deep grass to a tight pin. If the green is divided into two tiers, you're better off missing just off the green on the same side as the tier with the flag on it.

Let's use a famous par-5 as another example—the 13th hole at Augusta. It plays about 510 yards for the Masters—

very short by modern Tour standards. But it's not as simple as just bombing a drive out there and firing away with a 5- or 6-iron toward the green. The hole is a dogleg left, with a creek along the left side and trees and pine straw down the right. The green has different levels, and it's protected in front and on the right by water. Miss long into the swale or into the big bunker on the left there and you have a scary downhill shot to a different tier, with the shaved slope and the water in play.

Most players in the Masters field have the length to reach the green in two, but it hinges on the tee shot. The goal is to aim it down the right side of the fairway with a draw, trying to sling a driver or 3-wood around the dogleg and get to the flat area about 185 yards from the green. From there, they can play an iron shot with enough spin to hold the green, and hopefully get the ball to end up on the same tier as the flag. But fail to draw the tee shot enough and you'll end up in the light rough or pine straw on the right side of the fairway— with a tantalizing look at the green, but a sketchy lie and less potential to control the shot with spin. Overcook the draw and you're in the creek and taking a penalty drop.

Compare that to how the average member would potentially play the hole from 455 yards. Hit a stock 220-yard fade and you're looking at 230 yards to the flag—and 220 of it is carry. It is clearly a three-shot hole even on a career day. Instead of being discouraged by that fact, embrace it. It gives you a lot of strategy options and room to play the shots you like to hit.

If you fade the ball, hitting driver isn't going to be a comfortable shot on this dogleg left. So why not hit a 3-wood or even a hybrid—both of which curve less than a driver—and leave yourself 280 yards from the green? It's already a three-shot hole, so you're not giving anything away. Instead of laying up with a wedge, you can play a second shot with a middle iron to the right side of the fairway down in front of the creek, opening up the entire green for you to hit a full 9-iron or wedge shot in. You're also reducing the chance of hitting a really crooked tee shot with a longer club that would immediately set you scrambling to get back into position.

I finally learned how to play the 18th at Pebble Beach once I realized that I couldn't reach the green in two no matter how good of a tee shot I hit. After having the experience of twice being in the last group and hitting it out of play to give away the chance to win the Crosby, I changed my strategy. I decided to hit it at the edge of water on the left and cut it, and my shot ended up somewhere around the pine trees. Then I hit a shot up there to pitching wedge distance and took my chances with one of my favorite clubs. That took all the stress off me on that hole. I guess it was all those years playing with Bob Charles—who actually seemed upset when he hit a good tee shot on a par-5, because he was always so set on laying up to his favorite yardage. He knew what his strengths were, and he played to them.

If you simply make a conscious decision to picture the shot you want to hit and plan for it in your strategy and club-selection decisions, you're already going to be way, way ahead of the game. If you make a mistake and hit a poor shot, at least you'll have a chance to be in a more favorable area than you would if you just got up and whaled away at it with no strategy.

A good example of this is what happened to Phil Mickelson at the 2006 U.S. Open at Winged Foot. He had a one-shot lead going into the last hole—a 450-yard par-4. He hadn't been hitting his driver well all day, but he pulled that club again and hit a famously bad tee shot into the hospitality tents down the left side of the hole. That's not a big deal. Every player hits bad shots every once in a while.

It was what happened next that illustrates my point.

Phil's ball ended up in a trampled dirt area near the hospitality tents. The good news was that he could get a club on the ball. But instead of taking his medicine and punching out to the fairway and playing for a par or bogey, he tried to slice a hero 3-iron around a tree between himself and the green. It hit a branch and kicked back toward him, into more rough. He hit the next shot into a greenside bunker and ended up making a double-bogey to lose the tournament by a shot.

Phil's problem wasn't that he couldn't see the shots he wanted to hit. Heck, he's one of the most creative and talented players ever to play the game, and he legitimately believes he can pull off almost any shot—as he has numerous times. On the 13th hole at Augusta in 2010, he hit a huge cut from the pine straw over the creek and onto the green to set up an easy birdie—a shot many players wouldn't be brave enough to try. The problem at Winged Foot was that the risk did not outweigh the reward. Because of the front-left flag location on that hole, left was the one place you didn't want to miss off the tee. And if you hit it into the bunkers left of the hole—where Phil put his third shot—you were left with an extremely difficult downhill bunker shot.

After that first watery swing with my pro-am partner—the guy we talked about at the beginning of the chapter—I asked him what he saw when he was up on the tee. He told me he was looking at the flag. I asked him to take one more club, move to the other side of the tee box and picture his shot flying through the air with a nice fade, landing on the front of the green and rolling toward the hole. He went through his process, made a couple of practice swings picturing that specific shot and then got up and hit it. As the ball was in the air, I asked him if he'd ever seen a hole-in-one. "No," he said. "Well, you're about to . . ." I told him.

If you play the same course most of the time, you already know where all the most dangerous spots are on the hard holes. Think about all the big numbers you've made on those holes, and consider what would happen if you changed your approach to one where your goal was to set yourself up with a chance to get up and down from the fairway just in front of the green for par. Instead of swinging harder with the driver to get the ball down there closer on a long, hard hole, dial it back and hit a 3-wood or 5-wood and find the fairway. Instead of trying to hit a miracle hybrid 200 yards over deep bunkers in front of the green, hit a 6-iron to your favorite wedge distance and try to get up and down from there. If you don't, you've made a stress-free bogey and you can move on without wrecking your scorecard.

By the same token, if there's a part of your game you feel strongly about—like Phil does about his short game, or I do about my short game and putting—you can afford to take more risks. You're doing it when the odds are in your favor. For example, I always played with the belief that I could get up and down from virtually anywhere. I never hit the ball tremendously accurately off the tee, but when I found a fairway I was almost always aggressive—even for tucked pins.

Maybe the driver is the best club in your bag. If that's the case, you can take some risks launching it on shorter, tighter holes. If you don't curve the ball much, your mediocre shot might just trickle into the rough—but you'll be farther down the hole and playing a shorter club into the green.

Is there some rule of thumb or ratio that determines when to take a risk and when to play safe? I wish I could tell you that you can play by numbers that way, but I really believe it's more of a feel and confidence situation. Your mind and emotions are going to let you know if you're trying a shot outside your comfort zone. I want you to be standing over your next shot with a positive mind-set, seeing exactly how you believe it will turn out. You won't have much success if you're over the ball protecting against the shot you *don't* want to hit. In other words, you're doing it wrong if you're addressing the ball and your last thought is, "Whatever you do, don't go over there . . ."

When you *do* go over there, into the trees or any other trouble spot, what do you do then? PGA Tour players call it getting out of position on a hole, and your primary goal when you're out of position is to get back in position. That could mean playing for the green if you have a lie where the ball is sitting up and there's no obstacle in front of you. But more often it means playing some kind of safety shot back to the fairway.

If you do make the determination to get back into play, that isn't the time to get discouraged and lose your focus. I see a lot of players who take a quick, disinterested chop at the ball when they're playing out of the trees, just to move it forward. That simply prolongs the pain of the bad shot. When you're playing from the trees or some other problem area, you want to focus and make a mental picture of the shot just as you're learning to do with all the other shots from the tee, the fairway, or on and around the green. See the window you want the ball to fly through and the spot where you want it to land.

You also want to have a specific plan for the recovery shot you're hitting, so that you have the best chance on the next shot to get to where you want to be. It doesn't make any sense to punch out into a spot that's as bad or worse, or to lay up to a place where you have to hit from an awkward stance or from an in-between yardage.

Hole strategy doesn't end when you get to the short game and putting. In my last book, *Unconscious Scoring*, I talked about my strategy for shots around and on the green. I'll recap it briefly here in case you haven't heard about it. Players get in trouble around the green because they approach every shot as some kind of mixture between a high shot and low shot. They don't visualize exactly what they want the shot to do and where they want it to land, and they end up hitting an in-between shot with the hole as the target.

You can simplify your short-game strategy a ton if you

learn to hit two basic stock shots—a high shot and a low shot. After you check out your lie and where the pin is located, you then pick where you want your shot to land and choose the kind of shot that works best for the situation. If you're on fairway grass and have a lot of open green in front of you, you can hit a simple low shot. If you're in deeper grass, or need to carry an obstacle or land the ball on a tier, you can play a high shot. The strategy element comes in when you're deciding which shot to hit for the circumstances.

I find that about 75 percent of all the short-game shots I hit are low shots—running chips that are controlled with the left hand. On those shots, I'm picking a spot to land the ball on the green close to me, and reading the line like I would for a putt. Your strategy goals for a low shot are the same as they would be for a putt. You want to visualize the ball's entire route to the hole, along with the spot where it will enter the cup on the high side of the break.

The high shot, controlled by the right hand, is more appropriate when you have to carry an obstacle between you and the start of the green—deep grass, a bunker—or you don't have a lot of room on the green for the ball to roll out. The important strategy element to consider here is that it's much easier to play a slightly longer putt from the same tier on which the hole is located than it is to have a shorter putt from a different tier. That means that the hole isn't going to be your target on some shots. If you're playing at a flag that has a steep drop-off just behind it down to a different tier, you're going to want to give yourself a buffer. If that shot ends up just short of the hole, that's OK. The alternative is a really hard 25-footer up a slope—and an invitation to three-putt.

Strategy is about tilting the odds in your favor as much as you can. But don't lose sight of the fact that your ultimate goal is to get the ball in the hole. You're looking for that personal balance between playing it safe and standing over a shot believing you're going to hole it. Every time you put yourself in better position to hit a scoring shot, you're learning when to push that accelerator.

8

HOW TO PLAY
FOR BUSINESS

WHEN you're out playing late in the afternoon with a couple of friends, the course is wide open, and the weather is perfect, it's easy to relax and enjoy yourself. Those days are the best of what golf is all about.

But sometimes the stakes are a bit different than a friendly $10 Nassau.

One thing that sets golf apart from any other sport is the ability to mix in a business or meeting component. It's hard to hit the tennis court with your boss or your client and have a meaningful conversation. On the course, you're either walking or riding in the cart with somebody for four or five hours—and only about twenty minutes of that is spent actually hitting shots. That leaves lots of time for conversation—and making and forming an impression of somebody.

Even if you normally have a pretty calm and carefree temperament on the course, being onstage like that with a colleague, supervisor, or client for four or five hours at a stretch can be very stressful. Being able to take the temperature of the social or business situation and respond appropriately—both in how you interact with the other people in your group and how you actually play your game—isn't something you should automatically know how to do. It takes practice and guidance from somebody who has been there before.

If I had a business card, it would say: "Dave Stockton: Player, Motivator, and Instructor." For at least the last forty years, interacting with business people in client outings, clinics, and pro-am pairings has been just as big a part of my job as playing and teaching. I've done more than two thousand corporate outings since the late 1960s—and for a good number of years, those outings provided more of my income than tournament golf did. I'm proud of my record as a player—twenty-four victories on the PGA and Champions tours, including five majors—but I'm just as proud of my record in the corporate world. I might have been able to win more tournaments or contend for more majors if I had focused all of my attention on practicing and playing. But I've been able to help thousands and thousands of players, make great friendships with a wide variety of people, and provide a living for my family.

Does it help to be a naturally outgoing person? Sure. I love meeting new people. But I had to learn the corporate side of things. My first outing was in New Jersey, for TWA. I was supposed to be one of the secondary guys at the event, but the main person didn't show up, and I had to handle it myself. I went into it with the main goal of interacting with each person who was there and giving each of them something personal to take away and use on their own game. My approach is the same in the outings or clinics I do now—to give people a personal experience and to make them comfortable.

I love doing outings, and so do Ron and Dave Jr. They don't feel like work. If I have thirty people or a hundred people, by the time I'm done, and they're all rolling the ball so much better, it feels like I won a tournament. A lot of players don't like to do outings, and they talk about things that don't relate to the players who are sitting there. Our goal is always to help a player slice three or four shots off their handicap. If you cut a guy from a 12 to an 8, they're going to think that's the greatest thing in the world—and that you are, too.

After I did that first outing for TWA, they asked me back to do another one a few months later. They flew my wife and I from Hawaii to Portugal to shoot an in-flight movie. And when one of the executives left TWA to go to American, he signed me to represent them in what became a forty-year relationship. And the people I've been fortunate enough to meet along the way—actors, businesspeople, war heroes and even presidents—have just been amazing. I've been getting paid to hang out with President Gerald Ford, Willie Mays, Tom Selleck and Leonard Firestone. It's a tough gig to beat.

You don't have to be some kind of social butterfly to feel comfortable keeping up a business conversation on the course. When Ron and I started working with LPGA star

Yani Tseng four years ago, we had some things to sort out with her game. But after spending some time with her, it was clear to me that some of her issues came from a long-standing fear of the interaction and attention that comes with winning. She was nervous about interacting with sponsors because her English wasn't perfect. Annika Sorenstam suffered from the same anxiety—not because of her language, but because she was basically a shy person. But by the time Annika got to the end of her career, she had embraced the spotlight that comes with being the best player in the world—to the point that she played in a men's tour event and handled all the attention that came with it with grace and class.

I don't think anyone had sat down with Yani and just given her a simple breakdown of what to expect in the tournament-winner setting. We talked it over, and I tried to take away some of the mystery of it and give her a step-by-step process to prepare what she wanted to say—to the sponsors, the fans, and the media. It's one of the basic lessons I learned from the public-speaking courses my mom made me take when I was a teenager. If you prepare what you want to say and you know the format of what's coming next, you lose those fears of the unknown and of making a mistake in front of a bunch of people you don't know.

You might not be playing for a U.S. Open trophy, but a round of golf with an important client or the leader of your company is just as big, relatively speaking. It's easy to understand how the performance pressure that comes with wanting to do well with a business colleague can mix in a bad way with the regular mental stress that the game produces on its own.

Every time I play a pro-am round, I begin the day with the same mission. I want to make my guys comfortable, and try to get them in position to play better than their regular game. That's a tall order, because everything about the pro-am experience is different than a day-to-day round of golf for the average player. There's a tour player there, crowds of people lining the fairways, and a team format.

I make the format work for me. I'll remind the players that each of us only needs to count on four holes. If they do that, we'll shoot 20-under and have a good chance to win. My role is to be the team captain and chief motivator, and to get the players so engrossed in the team strategy and goals that they forget about the individual concerns they might have with their own games. I take them through my thought process for each hole, and I encourage them to ask as many questions as they like. For many of them, it might be the only chance they'll ever get to play with a tour player in a tournament setting, and I want them to get the most out of it. On the Champions Tour, there are two pro-ams—one on Wednesday, and one on Thursday. If my guys go out and shoot 12-under with me, and then go shoot 20-under the next day with another pro, I take a lot of pride in that. That means more to me than if we actually went out and won the thing. They're taking something home with them to help their game—and I'm getting something out of it, too. The guys who have always been world-class at working with people—like Phil Mickelson and Arnold Palmer—understand that dynamic. They're genuinely curious about people, and enjoy the time. The guys Phil plays with are learning about golf from him, and he's doing the exact same thing with the CEOs in his pairing—learning about the business world. It makes for a fun, comfortable day.

You can use variations of that same approach for your personal business round. Your mission should be to stay as close to your normal game as you can, and to make the conversation a two-way street. I realize that's easier to say than to do sometimes, but the right frame of mind is everything.

The first thing to remember is that you're going to be judged much more on your attitude and ability to hold a conversation than the quality of your game. People want to do business with people they like, and nobody likes the player who gets enraged about hitting a bad shot—or one who gives constant post-shot commentary about how he or she never usually plays so badly. As I said, your goal is to be yourself and be comfortable. A bad score isn't the end of the world, and it probably won't have any impact on the business you're trying to do. But you could shoot 69 and complain about missed putts, bad breaks, and the condition of the course and find yourself sitting alone at the 19th hole when you're done. I know of a handful of top PGA Tour players that you'd be excited to hear you were paired with in a pro-am, but that you wouldn't pay $5 to play with a second time because they made it clear that they had no interest in you or your game.

Don't be that guy or girl.

Your temperature-taking skills will really come into play when you're sizing up a business associate or client you've never played with before. You want to be yourself and play your own game, but you need to take some cues from your playing partner. Is this going to be a hardcore, competitive day for him or her, or is it more about having a few beers and enjoying being outside? Depending on your personality— and your wallet—you're naturally going to enjoy one kind of game more than the other, but the key is to be ready for whichever comes. If your partner hits two or three balls off the first tee and isn't interested in a money game, you're going to come across as tone deaf if you remind him or her to back up a few inches because he or she is hitting from in front of the tee markers. And if the other three players in the group want to play for a little something, you're going to stand out in a bad way if you beg off. I'm not suggesting you play for an amount outside your comfort zone—or the amount in your wallet—but try to go with it. Just make sure you get all the strokes coming to you!

Even if you're on the losing end, ask yourself if it's worth spending a few bucks to be in good with your boss or your client. The answer is almost always yes. Relax and enjoy yourself, and play to the best of your ability. Resist the temptation to miss a few putts to give away the match in the interest of making the other person feel good. I've found that most people want your honest effort and good company.

If you're in a position where your associates ask you to suggest a game, I think $5 four ways—one bet on the front, two on the back and one for the overall—is a good number. It's enough to keep things interesting, but you don't get beat up too badly even if you get swept. Guys like Phil Mickelson, Keegan Bradley, Raymond Floyd, and Lanny Wadkins always like to play for big money during practice rounds, because it gets their juices flowing and at least partially replicates tournament pressure. Personally, I always liked to use my practice rounds to hit shots to the places where I knew the flags were going to be during the tournament. You'll never see me playing for more than $5 four ways, because then it seems too much like work!

Years ago, I went over to Eldorado Country Club in Indian Wells to help President Ford with his game, and Bob Hope and an amateur friend of his were there. Bob immediately suggested we have a game, and he and President Ford partnered up against me and Bob's friend from Cincinnati. But the friend was so rattled to be playing with us—not to mention being accompanied by a contingent of Secret Service agents—that he was a complete nonfactor. On the front nine, the President made seven pars and a couple of quads, and Bob never missed a fairway. I shot 32, and the match was even. I ended up shooting 63, and we beat them 1-up to win ten bucks. We went back to President Ford's house for a drink, and I went through the scorecard. The amateur hadn't helped me with a single shot the entire day. I was just happy to get out of there alive. The President joked that he was never going to pay me my $10, and instead, gave me the actual gavel he used to bring Congress into session before he became president. I'm proud to have it here on the desk in my office.

9

HOW TO SHARE THE GAME

FROM my dad down through me and on to Ron and Dave Jr., we're a golf family. For more than seventy-five years, the Stocktons have been playing and teaching the game—and sharing it with thousands of players around the world.

I'm extremely proud to see my sons carry on the tradition started by my father. They're teaching many of the same principles my dad learned from Alex Morrison in the 1930s.

Our message has been consistent over so many years for a simple reason: It works. In the last four years alone, tour players we work with have won more than ninety tournaments—including all four majors on the men's tour, and six on the LPGA Tour.

I believe the reason we're able to connect with so many different kinds of players—from the PGA Tour to the LPGA

Tour to the average amateur in a one- or two-day clinic—is because we teach things that are intuitive and easy to understand. And when players see the simplicity of it, they start to feel and build on the confidence you need to play your best golf. It's just as true for a tour player as it is for somebody trying to break 90 or 100 for the first time.

And that's really the key to successfully introducing someone to the game—whether it's a junior player or an adult. Taking it one step at a time gives a new player the chance to experience some small victories. That was my dad's genius as a teacher. I was always pestering him for more information, but he knew that the game works best when you're not trying to crunch six or seven swing thoughts together in your head while you swing. My boys have followed that tradition, too, and it's how we all teach today.

When I introduced my own boys to the game, I was in a slightly different position than my dad. He was busy running a sporting goods store when I was a kid, so I didn't get a chance to play many full rounds with him. But he was never very far away and was able to give me day-to-day guidance. On the other hand, when I had a family, I was out on Tour. My kids could travel with us when they were small, but when it came time to go to elementary school, they obviously spent more time at home.

Still, my approach with them was similar to the one my dad took with me. We talked about the swing basics every player needs to know—things like grip and posture—but my lessons were more about picturing shots and learning scoring strategies. David showed a knack for it right away, especially around the greens. Ron developed a little bit more slowly. I actually think he would have preferred to play left-handed, but I opened the garage and told him that there were five thousand clubs in there and not one of them was for a lefty!

When they were seven or eight years old, I really pushed both of them toward team sports like soccer and baseball, so they could learn the positives and negatives of that dynamic. They learned how to get along with people and follow a coach's direction, but they also got a taste of what makes golf so great for an individual competitor. On a team, you could give 125 percent and not get a positive result because of somebody else's mistake. In golf, you're out there on your own. Nobody is responsible for your score but you.

In the summer, they'd come out on tour and we'd all travel together. I'd play four or five tournaments in a row, and they'd come from city to city. My wife, Cathy, deserves a huge amount of credit, because she was responsible for lining up interesting things to do in Milwaukee, Hartford, Flint, or any of the other cities we visited. When I won the PGA at Congressional in 1976, we spent all day Monday in Washington, DC, and went to the White House. The kids weren't buried in golf twenty-four hours a day, and I think that really helped keep their interest in it.

I was fortunate to have a long career on the PGA Tour and then transition to the Champions Tour, so the boys could be right there with me when they were old enough to come out and caddie. David carried the bag for me until he went to USC to play college golf, and then Ron took over. By that time, they were both very advanced, not only in what they knew about the golf swing, but also about how to play the game mentally.

David went on to have a successful college career—he finished second to Phil Mickelson in the NCAAs—and make the PGA Tour, and Ron led the nation in scoring at the University of Redlands. I could tell by David's sophomore year that he knew he wanted to play for a living. Ron is brilliant in so many ways that I don't think he would have ever gone into golf if I hadn't been a Tour player. He would have been great at something else. He's been able to organize all the philosophies we have into a coherent program because of the questions he's asked over the years—things that hadn't even occurred to me. Ron has been a terrific teacher for more than twenty years, and Dave has really blossomed in that department over the last five years, after finishing his playing career.

Obviously, you don't have to grow up in a golf family to get the right start in the game. I'm asked all the time how I would introduce a kid to the sport today, and a lot of my advice is the same as it was for my own kids.

As much as you want your child to love the game and become a player, you can't push anyone into something that doesn't suit them. When I was a kid, you had to be pretty inept at all the "action" sports to get into golf, but the game is filled with athletes now. That's why early exposure to a lot of different sports is important. Some people thrive on the camaraderie and teamwork aspect of baseball or football. Even if your child shows a lot of potential as a golfer, there's no reason to ever block him or her from playing other sports, if they're interested in them.

Most parents know the stories of parents like Earl Woods, who are instrumental in propelling their talented child to the highest levels of the sport. I'm not taking anything away from the job Earl did with Tiger—Tiger has said it was his father's guidance that made it possible for him to flourish through a variety of swing coaches and swing changes—but I'd argue that a vast majority of kids ultimately don't respond to getting pushed.

Up-and-coming talent Lydia Ko is a great example of what I'm talking about. Her parents have been great about supporting her and encouraging her in the game, but they've also let her live her life. She's out winning multiple pro events as an amateur, but she's excited about getting back to high school in New Zealand to see her friends. I hope it continues that way. Phil Mickelson and Arnold Palmer are two other great examples of talented players whose parents presented them with the opportunity and let them take the lead on what to do with it.

There's so much opportunity out there for talented kids to, at minimum, get a free college education. I can understand the pressure that parents are under when they're faced with writing those tuition checks, so the temptation to push a kid down a sports scholarship path is there. Coming down hard on a kid can produce some good tournament results in the short term, but it can definitely be harmful for a young person's long-term love for the game. The LPGA Tour has seen a lot of promising young Korean players whose parents rode them hard to early professional success, only to have the players burn out on the game at an early age. Handled the right way, this is a game for a lifetime—as it should be.

If your child can shoot scores in the 70s by the time he or she is thirteen or fourteen years old, it's reasonable to start thinking about scholarship golf. But the best path to the college game is getting sound instruction on both the mental and physical components of the game and on how to score—not just how to swing. The AJGA tournament circuit can be a great way to give your kid some exposure to the competitive part of the sport. It's so well organized now that it's almost a miniature version of the PGA Tour. Just make sure you're driving your kid around to those regional tournaments for the right reasons. It's about getting the junior player some experience and knowledge about his or her game, not about you achieving something vicariously through your child.

The most important piece of advice that I would give parents and aspiring junior players is the same one I'd give the die-hard 10-handicapper who plays two or three times a week at his or her club: You can't let your results on the golf course define who you are or how you feel about yourself. The game is just one part of your life—and that's true even if you ultimately play it for a living. Your last shot, last hole, last round or last season doesn't determine your self worth.

My dad wanted me to learn to play the game well, but it was more important to him that I had the values and tools necessary to lead a good life. He was giving me lessons in responsibility, patience, hard work, and the need to challenge yourself. He was showing me the importance of family and friends, and of doing things that you enjoy.

And that's really what this game is about. If you can impart that kind of love and enjoyment to somebody else, you've given them an incredible gift.

Acknowledgments

FROM the time I started playing, I've been fortunate to have wonderful guidance. It all started with my parents, Gail and Audrey Stockton. A lot of teachers can introduce a kid to the basics of the golf swing. My dad had a bigger plan. He taught me how to play the game, right from the beginning.

My dad always made it clear that the mind was the key to reaching my potential as a player. As I made my way through college and onto the PGA Tour, I met some important people who both reinforced that message and became wonderful, lifelong friends. I followed Al Geiberger at USC, and he was never anything but generous with his time and advice about surviving and thriving as a professional. I was lucky to have him looking out for me when I came out onto the tour, and it's been an honor to play with him—and against him—for more than forty years.

The tour could be a tough place for a young player. The money was a fraction of what it is now, and a lot of the veterans saw the next wave of players as a threat to their livelihood. The first time I was ever paired with Arnold Palmer, I stood on the first tee looking at the huge army of fans lining both sides of the fairway and just about had a heart attack. I had never seen so many people on a golf course. Don January was the third player in the group, and after we all hit away, he pulled me aside as we left the tee box. He told me to play my own game and to not let any of the hoopla surrounding Arnold get to me. I just had to go out there and play at my regular pace and not get sucked in to playing at lightning speed like Arnold always did. He also reminded me that I deserved to be out there. It came at exactly the right time, and I'll always be grateful for the kindness Don showed me.

When you play professional golf, you're always aware that your family back home is counting on you. I took that responsibility very seriously, and I arranged my schedule in a way that let me maximize my corporate events and outings. As time went on and I had more success as a player, I could have filled my whole off-season with corporate days if I had wanted to. But thanks to friends like Mike Hunt, I learned how important it is to approach all the things you do with a positive attitude. Otherwise, it's easy to get burned out. The first time I ever took a trip with Mike, I was coming off a stretch of really poor golf. On our second day of fishing, Mike asked me how old I thought he was. I guessed sixty-five, and he smiled and said seventy-seven. Then he said something I'll never forget—"God doesn't count the days you spend fishing." I adapted it by replacing fishing with golf, and that idea became a mental building block for me. It helped remind me that golf was a game and that I needed to enjoy myself doing it—and that helped keep me focused at the end of the long season.

I wouldn't be able to tell this story as a teacher without my sons, Ron and Dave Jr. Ron has a psychologist's mind, and his insights into how and why the things we teach work so well are a huge reason for the success we've had. He's the best teacher I've ever had. Dave Jr. has an incredible eye for the game. From the time he was a teenager caddying for me on the PGA Tour, he's had a knack for dissecting both golf swings and course strategy at an extremely high level. He knows both how and when to hit every shot in the bag—and can relate to anyone. I'm incredibly proud of both of them, and it's an honor to teach with them.

We couldn't do any of this without Cathy Stockton. She's more than a wife, a mother, a teacher, and a friend. She's the center of our family, and she's walked every step of the way with me from the day I turned pro in 1964. She's the greatest blind date in history.

Ralph Cross does far more than keep my business life organized. He's a trusted friend who knows that relationships with good people are the most important thing. He was responsible for getting me together with Matt Rudy, who helped me write this book, along with *Unconscious Putting* and *Unconscious Scoring*. Matt does an amazing job of capturing what I want to say and organizing it into what you see here. Farley Chase got us a great deal with Gotham, where Bill Shinker has always been a great supporter. And it was a pleasure to work with Brooke Carey for the first time.

I'm grateful to the PGA of America for giving me the Ryder Cup experience, both as a player and a captain. That organization has been a huge part of my life, and I'm extremely proud to represent it as a member. On the teaching side of things, I want to thank John St. Clair, Roger Cleveland, Paul Runyan, Chuck Cook, Mac O'Grady, Jim Flick and Tom Self. Clubfitter Mario Cesario was the first one to show me a picture of my swing. From our days in Westlake, I want to mention Clint Airey, Ron and Rick Rhoads and the whole Rhoads family, Mike Davis and Red Argue. And then there's Mike Dalton of Maui Jim, Mike and Barbara Gunn from American Airlines, the Lapuks from Hartford, Dr. Ed Powers from Boston, our Northern California cousins the Zimmerman clan, the Barts from Charlotte, NC, my trusted caddie Todd Newcomb, Jay and Marlene McConnell, Joe and Trish Patterson and Carol and Ken Williams. Many thanks to our Hawaii friends Pard Erdman and Guy Lamb, among others. I've met so many great people hunting and fishing, including Bev and Mike Karam and Rick Ochs. Deborah Graham gave me terrific insight on how the mind works. Among many others out on tour, I'm grateful to know Paul Azinger, Donna Caponi, Phil Mickelson, Rory McIlroy, Lee Trevino, Dale Douglass, Don Pooley, Morris Hatalsky, Payne Stewart, Christy O'Connor Jr., Annika Sorenstam, Morgan Pressel, Brittany Lang, Suzann

Petterson, Yani Tseng, Jay Sigel, Massy Kuramoto, Takaaki Kono, Dow Finsterwald and so many others. Laurie Hammer and I won the Haig & Haig together, when it counted as an official event.

I also want to thank some guys who show that strength in a much more important pursuit. In 2002, Jack Brown, the chairman of Stater Bros. Markets, invited Cathy and I to attend the Congressional Medal of Honor Convention in Riverside, California, and it changed our lives. Since then, I've been fortunate to be a part of the Stater Bros. Charities Dave Stockton Heroes Challenge charity event. It recognizes the heroic contributions made by these true heroes. It is truly an honor to have gotten to know some of these great men who have received our nation's highest honor, and we're all grateful for their service and sacrifice. It's been a pleasure to get to know men like The Hon. Ronald E. Ray, Jay Vargas, James Taylor, H. C. "Barney" Barnum Jr., Robert J. Modrzejewski, John F. Baker Jr., Robert Patterson, Salvatore Giunta and Joseph C. Rodriguez.

In closing, I want to dedicate this book to my very special friend Jim Langley, who passed away in July 2013. Jim had the finest character of anyone I ever met out on the tour, and he and his wife Lou have been an important part of our lives for more than forty-five years. Jim played under Coach Pete Newell on Cal's NCAA Champion basketball team in 1959 and went on to serve in the Marines afterward. After getting out of the Corps, he picked up a club for the first time in 1965, and the first professional tournament he ever played in was the tour qualifying school. He made it through, and as two California guys we became fast friends shortly after. Jim was the longtime head professional at Cypress Point. He and Lou were Ron's godparents—one of the best decisions Cathy and I ever made. He was a great man, and we're all going to miss him greatly.

INDEX